Measurement and Contr
Editor: T. P. Flanagan, OBE,

EXPERT SYSTEMS IN PROCESS CONTROL

By Janet Efstathiou

Longman

in association with
The Institute of Measurement and Control, UK

EXPERT SYSTEMS IN PROCESS CONTROL

First published 1989

Published by Longman Group UK Limited,
Longman Industry and Public Service Management Publishing Division,
Longman House, Burnt Mill, Harlow, Essex CM20 2JE, UK
Telephone: Harlow (0279) 442601

British Library Cataloguing in Publication Data
Efstathiou, Janet
    Expert systems in process control.
    1. Industries. Process control. Application of expert systems
    I. Title   II. Series
    670-42'7

ISBN 0-582-04267-4

Typeset by Page Bros (Norwich) Ltd
Printed and bound in Great Britain by
Bell and Bain Ltd., Glasgow

A welcome from the Institute of Measurement and Control

The Institute of Measurement and Control, the UK's chartered engineering institution covering the science and application of measurement and control technology, is interested in all techniques of measurement and control and recognises that the application of these techniques spreads across a range of process and manufacturing industries, as well as such areas as aerospace, power generation and distribution, and not forgetting the biomedical area. Its membership, on an international basis, is around 6000.

As such, the institute is dedicated to the furtherance and dissemination of knowledge of the theory, practice and potential of measurement and control technology throughout the UK, and throughout Europe and, indeed, in the world at large.

The institute, therefore, welcomes and commends the publication and objectives of the Measurement and Control Technology Series. The titles already announced cover some key areas of vital importance to industrial progress, efficiency and safety, and the titles under consideration indicate that an expanded series would be of equal interest.

The institute is pleased to note that the series editor is a former president, and that other members (including one other former president) are involved in individual volumes.

The institute wishes the series success. It will be of benefit to readers and their organisations. Applying the knowledge and increasing efficiency, safety and product reliability will be of benefit to the community at large, internationally. The institute's Royal Charter refers to the requirement to promote the science and practice of measurement and control technology for the public benefit. The series helps to do that and the institute is happy to be associated with it.

Michael Yates   January 1989
Secretary
Institute of Measurement and Control
87 Gower Street
London WC1

Series introduction

The subject of measurement and control is as broad as the whole of science and technology, and therefore, as in science and technology, most practitioners specialise in one or more aspects of the total field. Publications dealing with the current state of the art are therefore more effective as self standing reports on the specific topics which in total make up the general subject of measurement and control.

This series of books is aimed at summarising the state of knowledge and experience for specific topics in measurement and control technology. The topics may be well established, such as fluid flow measurement, or very new such as expert systems in process control. In each case the objective is to summarise the current state of knowledge so that the newcomer to the field is given the means whereby further experience can be more readily absorbed by a better understanding. Each book deals with the fundamental principles illustrated by examples of practical applications, and takes a look at likely future developments in the topic in the next decade or so. It also includes references for further reading, and contains information on organisations active in the field or through whom further information and experience may be obtained. The books in the series are not written as academic texts but do require degree standard knowledge. They will be ideal reading for science and engineering graduates entering the specific field and requiring, so to speak, to get up to steam as soon as possible. They are also aimed at the non-specialist technical manager requiring a sufficient knowledge of the field to make management decisions on applications or product development. This includes technical advisers making recommendations on measurement and control technology investment for financial investment institutions.

Terry P. Flanagan
Series editor

Tenterden, Kent
February 1989

Contents

Janet Efstathiou

Janet Efstathiou has been working on expert systems for almost a decade, while a lecturer at Queen Mary College (University of London) and at Cambridge University. She has always been interested in engineering applications of AI, such as process control and fault diagnosis of complex equipment, and has worked on several projects with a mixture of academic and industrial collaborators. She recently held a Royal Society/SERC Industrial Fellowship and is presently living in Oxford with her husband and two children.

Foreword

This book is intended to be read by engineers and software developers in various sectors of industry concerned with process control. It has grown out of experience working with and on expert systems for several years, as well as lecturing and teaching people what expert systems can do and are likely to be capable of doing in the future. The book was not written for undergraduate or graduate students, but they might find it a useful introductory text. Anyone else working in the area of expert systems might also find the specific requirements of process control provide an interesting contrast to those more usually discussed, such as medical diagnosis for example.

The book does not attempt to review every software product available and assess them for the process control industry. There are too many products, they change too frequently and each potential user has different requirements. Instead, this book aims to educate, so that the would-be expert system user would be in a better position to understand the technology, make a better decision about which projects to tackle, have a realistic idea of what they could hope to achieve and be aware of some of the difficulties of having an expert system accepted within their organisation. If the reader wants more information on products, the final chapter lists further sources of information.

I would like to acknowledge gratefully those colleagues over the years whose collaboration has contributed to the ideas behind this book. My students and colleagues at Queen Mary College have been very important, especially John Bigham, Soheir Ghallab, Meicy Halim, Costas Koukoulis, Mukta Krishnamurthy, Abe Mamdani, Kenji Sugiyama and Tsukasa Yamazaki. There are many more, too numerous to mention. I applaud them all.

Much of the material of the book has already been tested on people who attended one-day seminars on expert systems which were organised by Sira. I hope that they enjoyed them and found them useful. Certainly, I benefited greatly from the feedback which they provided. I'd like to thank Bill Simmonds and Chris Taunton for their help in those days, as well as granting permission to use some of their papers as source material for the case study in Chapter 8. However, the person who deserves particular thanks on that topic is Dave Haspel, lately of Blue Circle and now at Image Automation. His patient help and proofreading have been responsible for removing many of the flaws in my account of that project. Any remaining errors and ommissions are my responsibility alone. I pay tribute to Terry Flanagan, the series editor, and Colin Taylor at Longman, who have both been unfailingly helpful and encouraging. They have provided so much of the impetus.

Some of the chapters are extensions or summaries of articles that have already appeared elsewhere. I acknowledge the kind permission of Journal A (IBRA-BIRA), IEE Professional Publications and Pergamon Press. Full acknowledgements and references are in the References section.

I also acknowledge gratefully the support of the staff and colleagues at Cambridge University Computer Laboratory, who granted the facilities and environment in which to pursue the task of writing the book. To them, I owe much. Also, I would like most sincerely to thank Josie and Naomi Lucas and Lynne Wetton, whose help has been indispensable. They are the experts in control.

Janet Efstathiou   January 1989

Introduction

This report on Expert Systems in Process Control is a summary of how a particular aspect of Artificial Intelligence—Intelligent Knowledge Based Systems or Expert Systems—is being adapted and applied to the important task of industrial process control. Control Engineering has conquered many industrial automation problems, but a number of processes refuse to yield to classical control techniques.

In this book Dr Janet Efstathiou describes the principles behind the use of expert systems for controlling processes from knowledge bases which themselves are derived from the experience of skilled operators. She briefly outlines the history of expert systems and then concentrates on the rule-based methods which are particularly appropriate to process control. An explanation is given of how rules based on quantitatively vague terms like 'high', 'medium', 'low' can be handled effectively by fuzzy set theory and shows how the knowledge of the process operator can be represented in this way. Dr Efstathiou illustrates the principles by applying them to the imaginary but realistic case of a chocolate biscuit factory. She deals with the subjects of inference and knowledge acquisition and then describes as a detailed case study the application of the LINKman system to the control of cement manufacture, a notoriously difficult process to control by classical techniques. She finally deals with the topic of project selection, and gives a useful guide to the many organisations active in or having information on the subject of expert systems in process control.

Terry P. Flanagan
Series editor

Tenterden, Kent
February 1989

To

George
and
Mukta

Chapter 1 Process control and Artificial Intelligence

Artificial Intelligence (AI) has been a controversial subject in the UK for many years. With the publication of the Lighthill Report in 1973, AI was condemned as the refuge of a few cranks, frustrated by their masculine lack of ability to bear children, and establishing a 'pseudomaternal' relationship with their robots (p 7, Lighthill Report). The USA was not inhibited by such views and AI research continued. Meanwhile, improvements in hardware and software engineering made many AI techniques feasible and available to a mass market. So, in the early seventies, with the appearance of the first expert systems, AI began to move from the research lab into industry and gain a degree of respectability. Government initiatives in the early eighties supported and encouraged high technology, including AI and expert systems, such as Alvey in the UK, Esprit in Europe and the Fifth Generation programme in Japan. Companies in the USA pooled their efforts to establish pre-competitive research as well. Suddenly, AI was fashionable again. Expert systems were part of the excitement.

Expert systems grew from research in AI and so still retain that association. The slightly dubious air of AI, together with the popular science fiction images of robots taking over the world, create a sense of unease around expert systems. Combine this with the suspicions about computers taking over jobs and causing disasters and the whiff of controversy develops into a strong aroma of doubt.

The purpose of this introductory chapter is to discuss some of those doubts. The position of AI within perfectly respectable fields of engineering will be examined, together with its connections with philosophy and psychology. Much important and useful work is being done in psychology and philosophy on the future of AI, but we shall be concentrating on what AI and expert systems can do now. The orientation of this book will be pragmatic and this chapter is intended to orient the reader to that way of thinking about AI.

1.1 What is AI?

It will not come as much of a surprise to learn that Artificial Intelligence is a topic that defies definition. Intelligence is difficult enough to define and measure, but what can we reasonably expect of a machine before it could be agreed that the machine could be described as intelligent?

One definition of AI goes something like: Artificial Intelligence is the attempt to construct computer models of the human mind, based on our understanding of neurology, in order to reproduce some features of human behaviour.

The above definition places AI within the domain of psychology, with its focus on the use of the computer as a simulation device, which can help in research in understanding the brain. Work with this sort of goal is sometimes known as 'strong AI', because it is attempting to create intelligence which is artificial, exactly as the words mean.

Another approach to AI goes like: Artificial Intelligence is a collection of computer-based techniques, based on the manipulation of symbols rather than numbers, which enable computers to produce behaviour which resembles that previously only seen in humans.

This definition describes so-called 'weak AI' but the goals implicit in this definition are quite different from those of strong AI. Strong AI is focussed on understanding the mechanisms within the human brain, but weak AI says 'OK, let's take these symbol manipulation techniques and use them to do things like learning, reasoning about devices and making plans.' It is the case that since the only other things we know that can do these things are called intelligent, so in a way would be the computers that could also do these things. But reproducing human behaviour is not the goal of weak AI. While acknowledging that human intelligence is a marvellous and subtle thing, there are lots of things that humans do not do very well, especially when they are tired or stressed or have to cope quickly with quantities of data. So, although the techniques might produce behaviour that superficially resembles that of a human, the techniques can be applied and improved to yield behaviour that is quite beyond what we could expect of a human. And the techniques and algorithms could evolve so that their behaviour resembles human behaviour less and less.

These two approaches to AI parallel the way that the subject has been developing and is likely to develop in the future. On the one hand, strong AI will remain the activity of some psychologists, neurologists and physicians. Weak AI will turn into a collection of tools that will be applied by software, production and design engineers as they attend to the business of manufacturing products as efficiently as possible.

Although the two strands of AI will start to evolve separately, that does not imply that they will have nothing to share. The engineer's AI techniques will still owe their inspiration to studies of the mind. And the efficient application of the techniques will need to take into account the strengths and weaknesses of the human part of the team.

Let us understand this division of activity by looking at an

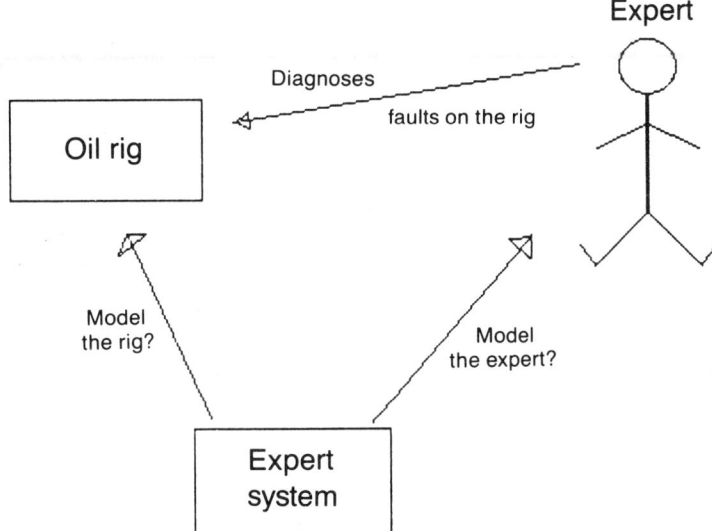

Figure 1.1 High AI could represent the expert's heuristic problem-solving behaviour, or construct a symbolic model of the plant and reason about it

example, such as the diagnosis of faults on an oil rig (*see* Figure 1.1). An oil rig is a complex piece of equipment, with automatic controllers to hold the flow of oil and gas to the desired levels and many sensors to measure flows and pressures etc. When a fault develops on the rig, the human operators are the only ones who can diagnose what is wrong and fix it. This ability to fix the fault is usually adequate, but if several faults develop at once, or they make a mistake and fix the wrong fault, then the outcome can be very serious. Worse, when some faults start to develop, they happen faster than the ability of the operators to reason about them, so without automatic safety mechanisms the whole rig can get out of control.

How can AI help? Strong AI would say 'Represent the human operator's knowledge about the rig. Try to capture his/her inference procedures and we can produce a computer that behaves almost exactly like the human operator.' Fair enough, but who wants a computer that panics? Weak AI says 'Let's make a symbolic model of the rig on the computer. We can represent how material flows round within the rig and how the various devices on board go wrong. We can ask the operators about the shortcuts they use to find faults and build them in too. Then we can wire it up to the control panel and it can let the operators know as faults begin to develop. It could also help clear some of the faults, suggest test and repair procedures, arrange partial or complete shut-downs and start the whole thing up again, but that all depends on what you're comfortable with.'

This description is unashamedly partial, but it makes the point. As illustrated in Figure 1.1, strong AI tries to capture the expert's exact expertise in the expert system. This leads to all sorts of interesting problems about the nature of knowledge, what does an expert know, what does the expert know that he/she knows, how can we find out what the expert knows, how can we make a computer know and do exactly the same? These are fascinating problems and computers are the perfect tool for researching them. But they are a distraction to the engineer, who wants to emulate the good bits of the expert's behaviour, and improve on the rest.

The weak AI solution would be to construct symbolic representations of the rig and acquire data automatically from the rig's sensors, similar to the control panel. The knowledge and data would be manipulated using techniques inspired by human behaviour, which has a very important effect. It is unlikely that we shall see the control of complex and dangerous manufacturing plant being entirely given over to computers for a few more years. The human operator will retain a role, as supervisor or overseer for some time. Therefore, the expert system's conclusions about the state of the plant and the recommended actions need to be presented to the human operator, via a user interface. The design of this interface is now the crucial link in the chain of control from operator to rig. If the inference and knowledge representation techniques that the computer uses have some resemblance to those of the human, then it is likely that the expert system's conclusions can be rendered understandable to the human, and that this can be done quickly enough to be useful in emergency conditions.

So, the weak AI approach to designing expert systems takes techniques inspired by psychology, but then transfers them to computer, with improvements to the efficiency of the algorithms. Weak AI then concentrates on the technological problems of coping with incoming data in real-time, how to form and test hypotheses and how to keep track of what is happening in the world. This is separate but related to the problems of designing the human computer team, so as to best exploit their separate and joint abilities. This includes the design of the interface and where to draw the line between what activities should be retained by the human and what entrusted to the machine.

The evolution of a shared responsibility betweeen human operator and expert system is entirely appropriate and to be expected. In the early days, expert systems were regarded as a source of conflict. Their proponents saw them as capturing the knowledge of and eventually replacing domain experts. The opponents were shocked at the presumption of computers which tried to emulate their behaviour. As the strengths and weaknesses of expert systems have been investigated, so it has become more acceptable to both parties to share out the tasks in an optimal way. The pendulum has swung from the one extreme to regarding the expert as god, to regarding the expert as mere knowledge-base fodder, but is now settling towards a middle ground of the expert and computer as team.

When this attitude to expert systems has taken hold, then expert systems will disappear. That is not to say that they will no longer exist. Instead, they will take on many different guises, evolving to fit many different niches and performing a huge variety of simple and complex tasks. They will become like any other software package or specialised piece of hardware, accepted for the job it does. Everyone will wonder what all the fuss was about.

1.2 Where does AI help industrial control?

There are two main ways in which AI is being used to help in industrial control. These will be distinguished as High AI and Low AI.

Low AI acts as an adjunct to existing techniques for process control. Automatic controllers need to be carefully tuned, which is a skilled and time-consuming task. Control engineers are expert at tuning and so expert systems may be set up to help the engineer in this time-consuming task. The basic, mathematical techniques of control engineering are not really disturbed in any way by this use of expert systems, which are used merely to help automate the implementation and maintenance of control.

High AI, by contrast, seeks to replace some of the tasks of current automatic control, by taking a fundamentally different appproach to industrial control. This is summarised in Table 1.1. It will never be the case that all of the existing techniques will be supplanted by AI-based techniques, but there are several tasks that existing techniques do not do very well, and which AI is likely to improve upon.

Existing approaches to control are based on complex mathematical techniques, using quantitative models of the process. In some industries, such models simply do not exist, despite many years of trying. Artificial Intelligence takes the approach of relying not on numerical methods, but symbolic computation. Knowledge about the process and plant is represented as facts, networks and rules, instead of differential equations. Instead of solving

Table 1.1 High AI, low AI and mathematical control

Criterion	High AI	Low AI	Numerical methods
Computational methods	Mostly Symbolic	Symbolic to assist numerical	Numerical
Knowledge representation	Rules, facts etc., in separate knowledge bases	Most likely as rules in separate knowledge bases	Equations embedded in programs
Likely user	Trained process operator	Control engineer	Control engineer

equations, the knowledge is used to reason about what goes on in the plant, how things fail and what the goals and constraints of the manufacturing process are and should be.

As manufacturing plant grow larger and more complex, the ability of personnel to control, maintain, schedule and plan how to operate the plant diminishes. The complexity of the plant is greater than they can handle effectively. There is no doubt that computers will play an ever increasing role in industrial control in the future. However, people will not be replaced altogether and so we need to design computer-based control so that it can be trusted and maintained by the personnel. This means that techniques which are effective in planning and control, but which have the additional property of being readily understood by the personnel are likely to have an advantage in effectiveness. Large, complex, manufacturing plants are here to stay and we need to pay attention to how they are going to be run by people and machines.

As plant become more complex, so the number of ways in which they can go wrong becomes impossibly large. It is not possible, therefore, to predict them all and lay down contingency plans for what to do when faults occur. However, as computer power increases, it becomes feasible to reason on-line, in real time, about what has gone wrong and what to do. Quantitative techniques do not have access to the right sort of knowledge about the plant and its components to be able to tackle fault diagnosis, test generation and plant shutdown. These are vital tasks in the future of industrial control. Increased environmental concerns and the production and treatment of hazardous material mean that safety will become more important, and more difficult to guarantee as plants become larger. It would be folly to rely on human beings alone to cope with the stress and danger of emergencies. AI-based techniques offer the most hopeful approach to tackling these problems.

The answer to the question at the start of this section would be as follows: Artificial Intelligence can provide a fresh outlook on the problems of industrial control. Some tasks, such as planning, scheduling, startup and shutdown, are already being solved by AI. Numerical methods for process control can be assisted by expert systems which help select, design and tune the best controller for a particular job. Furthermore, AI can provide techniques to control processes where numerical methods are less successful.

The answer above contains elements of both high and low AI. The two approaches are fully compatible. The current trends in hardware and software engineering, such as networking and object-oriented programming, are going to make it easier to combine numerical and symbolic methods of computation. Customised chips, optimised for their task, are going to speed up computation, so that processing power will make many things possible.

1.3 Plan of the book

Chapter 2 focuses on expert systems and industrial control, giving a definition of what expert systems are and where they fit in to the tasks of industrial control. This helps to define the particular areas that this book will address so that the reader may be forewarned about which techniques are best suited to particular types of problem.

Chapters 3 and 4 go into some detail about knowledge representation and inference in expert systems. Although rule-based systems are the main area of attention, other kinds of knowledge-based systems are described briefly to give the reader an idea of options that might be explored in the future.

Chapter 5 reinforces the work on knowledge representation and inference with an extended example on a fictitious chocolate biscuit factory. This is intended to show some of the ways in which expert systems may be used and to introduce the technical problems behind the screen.

Chapter 6 discusses how expert systems may interact with the outside world, both via sensors and with the user. Real-time systems are different from most of the better known applications of expert systems, so we look at another real-time system, the mobile robot, and see what lessons may be learnt from how it interacts with the world. Up-to-date examples of process control expert systems are also described briefly and discussed.

The first applications of expert systems to process control, in the early seventies, used fuzzy reasoning. Chapter 7 explains how fuzzy reasoning works and its role in rule-based control. Some variations on the theme of fuzzy rule-based control are also described briefly. Chapter 8 is an extensive case study on the application of these techniques to the cement industry, based on the experiences of Blue Circle plc.

Chapters 9 and 10 cover some of the practical issues of constructing and installing an expert system. Chapter 9 reviews some of the methods for acquiring the knowledge that forms the core of the expert system. Chapter 10 gives advice on how to select a problem that is likely to be tackled successfully by expert system techniques.

Chapter 11 returns to the broader picture to review some of the possible future applications of AI in industrial control.

The book concludes with a chapter of notes and references. Sources of information, such as trade associations and suppliers, are included, as well as references to useful books and papers.

Chapter 2 Introduction to expert systems

2.1 Introduction

As indicated in the previous chapter, there are several ways in which expert systems can contribute to process control. This book takes the 'high AI' (Artificial Intelligence) road, and will show that expert systems can be used to replace many of the tasks of mathematically-based process control. This is in contrast to the 'low AI' road, which leaves the mathematical controllers intact, but employs artificial intelligence to help in the design and tuning of those controllers. This does not imply that the two approaches are mutually exclusive. Technological advances will be made, driven by AI, and experience will show which tasks are best suited to which approach. It might turn out that some difficult problems that have resisted solution by mathematical controllers might yield to AI. As a result of the process knowledge gained thereby, mathematical control may be eventually applied. However, there are some problems, such as devising plans for emergency shutdown and start-up that are unlikely ever to be solved by mathematical methods and will require symbolic computation, as in AI.

All this requires a different way of thinking about control. It is important therefore to set the scene properly. This chapter introduces the basic ideas of expert systems and describes their evolution and benefits to industry. Many of the early expert systems were developed to help physicians diagnose medical cases, so we contrast the skills of process control with medical diagnosis to establish some of the requirements of expert systems in process control. Having oriented the reader to an AI style of thinking, we take a look at some of the tasks of industrial control and outline how AI can contribute. The main thrust of the remainder of the book will be towards low-level control and fault diagnosis, so the chapter concludes with a discussion of the styles of expert system required for these kinds of domain.

2.2 What is an expert system?

Many possible definitions exist of expert systems. Indeed, as the technology has become fashionable, many software products claiming to be expert systems are appearing.

In its simplest form, an expert system need consist of nothing more than a collection of knowledge, known as a knowledge base,

*Figure 2.1 A first generation
expert system*

The computer has a knowledge base, with an inference engine to manipulate the
knowledge and data. The user interacts with the expert system via a screen and
keyboard, in some ways similar to consulting an expert.

and a program which uses data from the outside world to derive
conclusions from facts in the knowledge base. This program is
known as the inference engine (*see* Figure 2.1). Many of the earliest
expert systems were constructed according to this plan.

The most striking thing about the knowledge base is style of
representation of the knowledge. Most programmers are familiar
with a procedural approach to programming. Knowledge, ie
programs, are written as algorithms or recipes, containing loops
and branches, but always with an ordering of the steps of the
program. The computer is expected to execute each statement in
turn, one after the other, according to the order they come in the
program, unless directed otherwise by statements within the
program itself. By contrast, the knowledge in the knowledge base
is represented declaratively. The order in which the facts occur is
not so important.

To take a well-known example, consider the knowledge needed
to colour a map so that no adjoining areas have the same colour.
The knowledge could be stated declaratively as:

> The map's regions are described by a relation *next-to*, where
> *next-to*(area1, area2) means that area1 and area2 share a
> common border.
> The requirement that: If two areas are next to each other, Then
> the colours used must be different.
> The set of colours to be used, say red, green, blue and yellow.

Note that this description contains no procedural information about how to colour the map. Changing from a procedural approach to knowledge representation to a declarative is often a big hurdle for programmers.

Maintaining the distinction between knowledge and the programs which manipulate it reflects modern software engineering practice. Since it is to be expected that the collection of knowledge available within an expert system will be subject to updating and modification, it makes sense for that knowledge to be altered as easily as possible, ie without having to go through a cycle of program editing and compiling. It is more efficient to represent and store the knowledge separately from the programs that manipulate it, maintaining a sort of knowledge-independence.

However, an expert system which consisted of nothing more than an inference engine and knowledge base would be unlikely to be acceptable in practice. The users of such an expert system would be unwilling to believe the conclusions presented by an expert system without some explanation of how those conclusions were reached. Some definitions of expert systems include the proviso that the expert system must be able to explain its line of reasoning.

Given that the inference engine and knowledge base are entirely separate, then it should be possible to empty the knowledge base and insert knowledge from an entirely different domain of expertise. The empty expert system was often referred to as a 'shell'. However, it has become apparent that it would not be easy to just replace one corpus of knowledge with another from a different domain to produce a new, working expert system. Practice soon showed that different domains of expertise had their own particular styles of reasoning associated with them. Some domains had special features that made them difficult to suit to the simple shells, such as time-dependence, feedback and level of uncertainty. More recently, shells have become more specialised in recognition of the variety of domains and their inference techniques. The opinion is beginning to form that the distinction between knowledge and inference is less clear cut than was at first believed.

As expert system technology evolves, so the expert systems themselves have become more complex and specialised. The knowledge has become more structured, involving deep, commonsense knowledge, as well as the technical knowledge of the expert. Programs have been added to make easier the tasks of constructing and maintaining the knowledge base, as well as providing various methods of interacting with it. Specialised software toolkits have been developed to assist in the construction of complex expert systems. Expert systems obtain their data from a variety of sources, apart from the user, such as sensors, databases and simulation programs. The term 'Intelligent Knowledge-Based Systems' is often used to cover these complex systems.

It is important at this stage to clarify the difference between the knowledge and data that are required within an expert system. First, there is the domain knowledge. This is the expert knowledge about a particular domain that would be valid each time that the expert system is used to solve a problem within the confines of the specified problem. So, if an expert system is constructed to identify faults on a given machine, that expert system might have general knowledge about the general properties of that type of machine, which would apply to every machine of that model. Also, the expert system might be tailored to cope with the individual idiosyncracies of the particular instance of the general machine and to represent details of the tasks to which that specific machine is applied. Compared to this is the data, taken from the world, which define a specific consultation with the expert system. So, on a particular day, the observed performance of the machine and its immediate history will be different each time the expert system is used to help diagnose a fault.

2.3 What does it look like? The roles played by expert systems in industrial control

In the previous section, we described how expert systems have adapted to the kinds of domains within which they operate. Not only have expert systems evolved to suit the kinds of knowledge and inference styles of the various domains, so they have evolved to suit their users and experts.

The original mode of interaction with an expert system was commonly via a keyboard. The system would pose questions on the screen to which the user was expected to furnish a reply. Depending on the domain, the user might be required simply to provide some personal details, or for an equipment diagnostic system, the user might be asked to carry out a test procedure or repair action and report on the observed effect. Whatever the domain, the system was in control of the interaction, in that it asked the questions and the user obediently answered, without any scope to volunteer information and limited ability to shortcut the questions that were being asked, even if it occasionally meant repeating answers that had already been provided earlier in the consultation.

The variety of roles played by an expert system may be best considered in relation to the expert. Some expert systems take over part of the expert's tasks altogether, whereas others fulfil the role of the humble helper. In process control, the human operator may have many of his routine tasks carried out by an expert system, bringing about an increase in the automation of manufacturing plant. Other experts might not be so easily displaced, for many possible reasons, ethical, moral or financial. For example, it is likely that people would not like to entrust the diagnosis of their ailments entirely to a computer-based expert system, even though the expert system might be able to outperform the familiar GP, with its repository of knowledge about exotic and unusual diseases that the GP is unlikely ever to encounter. So, for many experts and clients, the expert system would be acceptable as a meek assistant, subject to the control of the expert user. In these cases, the interaction between user and expert system is likely to follow a mixed initiative, with both user and expert system providing data or intermediate conclusions each time something interesting comes to light, whether as a result of the human professional's consultation with the client or during the system's process of inference.

2.4 What is it for? The advantages of expert systems

The construction and maintenance of expert systems within an organisation can be expected to lead to changes in how the organisation carries out its business. The introduction of expert systems resembles the introduction of any new technology, so it is best to regard expert systems as another technological advance, without being frightened by them. Most new technologies are accompanied by fears of loss of employment in particular, but like most of the rest, expert systems are more likely to lead to changes in jobs, instead of losses, with improvements in productivity and management. Some reasons for considering expert systems could be:

- retain skills in case people resign or retire;
- train new members of staff;
- multiply expert skills for use in other times and places;
- improve quality of fault diagnosis and repair;
- reduce likelihood of accidents;
- reduce plant downtime and material wastage;
- review and refine expert knowledge;
- carry out experiments to find optimum procedures;
- construct quick and easy prototypes;
- take over the operators' routine tasks;
- improve product yield and quality;
- better management.

Within an organisation, experts are the knowledgeable people with valuable skills. Their skills need to be passed on to other members of the organisation to ensure its continued functioning. For example, a vital piece of equipment might be maintained by one person only, because all the others who were trained at the same time have retired or left and the equipment suppliers no longer support training on that device. So what happens when the one and only expert fitter approaches retirement?

Expert skills are in short supply and heavy demand. When the expert is on holiday or on another shift, the performance of the organisation is affected. Human heads are a very fragile container for expertise if the organisation depends upon it. An expert system can multiply the expert's skills, so that the expertise is available at other times and places, when the expert cannot be present. Thus, an expert system for fault diagnosis can help reproduce the performance of the company's best maintenance engineer at all the company's factories around the world, day and night, 365 days per year. What's more, the performance of the expert system will always be consistent, which is very important for low-level control.

Studies of major industrial accidents have shown that many can be attributed to the compounding together of several minor faults, which in turn can be attributed to poor maintenance. Expert systems can help the fitter diagnose faults better and help ensure that the maintenance procedures are carried out properly.

Experts make mistakes, and naturally they will disagree. The construction of an expert system can provide an opportunity to identify the areas of disagreement. An expert system will always provide the same answers in the same circumstances, so there is an opportunity to carry out experiments to see which policy performs best.

Expert systems are finding a new role as a quick and easy way to develop prototypes. Rather than coding up a bespoke system, an expert system shell can be used to gather knowledge quickly and test it out on the problem. This can give a cheap and quick way to tackle a problem. If the performance of the expert system is adequate, then it can be left to do the job, or it can serve as the basis for a faster and better integrated, complete system. Furthermore, although it might be theoretically possible to implement a properly optimised control system, the cost of doing so might not be justifiable and so a suitable expert system could provide a better return on investment.

In some cases, the operators might know how to optimise the yield of the plant, but are unable in practice to do so, because of other demands on their time or safety considerations. An expert system could help here by encapsulating the optimum control procedures and executing them automatically, under the supervision of the human operator.

These reasons may be summarised as better management, through higher quality product and reduced downtime. The resources of the plant are more efficiently used, both the raw material input and the fixed equipment itself.

2.5 Historical development of expert systems

Expert systems have been investigated within Artificial Intelligence for about fifteen or twenty years. One of the first expert systems was MYCIN, which diagnosed bacterial infections, using rules like:

IF (1) The site of the culture is blood, and
    (2) The identity of the organism is not known with certainty, and
    (3) The stain of the organism is gramneg, and

(4) The morphology of the organism is rod, and
(5) The patient has been seriously burned.
THEN There is weakly suggestive evidence (0.4) that the identity of the organism is pseudomonas.

Since the rules do not apply in every case, but were more like plausible guides to reasoning, they contained a certainty factor. The certainty factors were manipulated in a fairly ad hoc manner, borrowing from both probability theory and fuzzy reasoning.

In practice, MYCIN was slow to execute, taking several minutes to suggest a diagnosis, but additions were made to the MYCIN suite of programs. TEIRESIAS was added to help the expert add rules to the knowledge base and EMYCIN (Empty MYCIN) was created. EMYCIN was MYCIN with the rules taken out, leaving the skeleton framework for knowledge representation and inference behind. This meant that EMYCIN could be tried on any fault diagnosis problem in any domain and was no longer restricted to its original medical subfield. EMYCIN was one of the first expert system shells, a computer program, with a built-in expert system structure, which could enable anyone to write an expert system.

Another early expert system, DENDRAL, used a different inference mechanism than MYCIN, reflecting a difference in problem-solving approach within the two disciplines. DENDRAL suggested structures for chemical compounds given data on their mass spectrometry fragments. The shells describe a model of the world, which may be more or less adequate for solving a particular problem. EMYCIN is better suited to medical problems, because they have the property of varying fairly slowly over time, compared to computation time-scales, and the decisions which are recommended are administered by a doctor, who could amend the therapy if required. For different domains, where fast or automatic response is required, say in fault diagnosis for a nuclear or chemical plant, the EMYCIN approach would not work.

It had been originally hoped that the inference mechanism would be domain independent, ie that changing the knowledge base alone would produce another expert system. Applications studies seem to indicate now that differences in applications and problem-solving styles demand shells which are to some degree tailored to the domain.

Another important expert system from the early days was PROSPECTOR, which was used to help identify geological formations. This used a Bayesian inference technique, which required the expert to assess prior and posterior probabilities for the likelihood of a hypothesis under the presence or absence of particular pieces of evidence.

DEC collaborated with researchers at Carnegie-Mellon University to build R1, an expert system to configure VAX computer systems from a customer's order. This has been installed very successfully and has now replaced the earlier manual configuration procedure. R1 contains about 2500 rules and is written in OPS5, a special language for executing production rules.

The early expert systems were sometimes capable of impressive performance, leading to some over-estimation of their potential. Expert systems shells were sold vigorously, with each claiming to be general purpose. There were obvious differences between the shells and the expert systems that they could be used to construct, with some being more suitable to kinds of problems than others. The debate shifted from the choice of shells to deeper questions about the nature of the knowledge that was required in different domains and the inference tools that were needed. Instead of the simple shell type of inference engine and a standard knowledge representation format (usually rule-based), enquiry began on the more complex kinds of knowledge-based systems that would be needed, incorporating deep knowledge and various inference techniques. Some specialisation began to develop as a morphology of domains emerged.

Associated with this movement in knowledge representation and inference, more attention began to be paid to the needs of the user of the expert system, who hitherto had been regarded as a dumb interface with the outside world, whose only function was to supply data and carry out some straightforward tests and repairs. User modelling created some interest, so that the expert system could adjust its user interaction strategy with the level of sophistication that could be inferred from the user's performance at the terminal. Mixed initiative strategies were developed so that the user and system could both volunteer information or suggest problem solutions for criticism.

The historical beginnings of expert systems in the medical domain have coloured the development of expert systems ever since. The particular needs of different domains are being realised now and expert systems are evolving to fill the particular niches. In the next section we shall point out the important features of industrial control by contrasting its requirements with those of medical diagnosis.

2.6 Industrial control and medical diagnosis

Many domains have been investigated by developers of expert systems, from medical diagnosis to situation assessment for the military. There have been several examples of expert systems constructed within the broad area of industrial control and it is instructive to examine the features of industrial control which distinguish the construction of expert systems within this area.

One of the most important features of industrial control is that the problem is bounded, or may be bounded. For example, an expert system, may be constructed to diagnose faults on a particular plant component, or to assist in the development of plans for a factory within a specified model of the world. The Knowledge-Based System (KBS) is targeted on a particular component, within a specified environment. Within these boundaries, certain classes of behaviour may be understood.

The industrial plant has been designed and constructed by humans, with a degree of complexity which could be handled, perhaps at various conceptual levels, by human operators and managers. The degree of complexity at any conceptual level may be chosen by the people who operate the plant. The complexity of the plant may be increased by other factors, such as variation in the behaviour of individual plant components or operators. For example, one machine may not be able to operate to all specifications or may be prone to breakdown if operated for too long a continuous period. Also, the manufacturing process itself which is being controlled may not be understood in great detail, although sufficiently well at an heuristic level for human operators to be capable of controlling it.

Contrast this with the medical diagnosis problem, where, although the problem may be bounded by coping with a particular patient, that patient's environment may not be well known, and indeed it may not even be known which factors may be important in diagnosing the patient's complaint. The mechanisms which are involved in the development of certain diseases are not understood, and statistical information on case histories, influenced by unknown factors, may be all the information the diagnostician has available. At least in industrial control, the behaviour of components may be isolated. Experiments may be performed and the contributing factors isolated, faily obviously in some cases, without compromising medical ethics.

Offsetting these advantages in industrial control is an important disadvantage – the effect of time. Medical diagnosis systems are often designed with the assumption that the state of the patient will not vary during the process of consultation. Generally, a patient's symptoms remain fairly stable during a doctor's examination. However, in fault diagnosis for industrial control, the fault may be developing rapidly while the diagnostic process progresses, perhaps causing other problems along the production line, leading to a cascade of faults. This property of faults is alone sufficient to make industrial control more complex, but there is a second way in which time complicates fault diagnosis.

During fault diagnosis, the operator may be asked to carry out tasks which affect the state of the plant, such as adjusting valve settings or temporarily switching flows on or off. These activities change the state of the plant from the original unknown state from which diagnosis commenced. Such activities could mean that a fault is diagnosed and cured during the consultation. On the other hand, if more than one fault is present, the KBS should be able to take account of the changes that have already been brought about when it proceeds to seek any secondary faults.

The doctor or consultant who is responsible for diagnosing disease is a highly skilled specialist, with several years' medical training, covering the physical reasons for disease and the process of accumulating evidence in support of particular diagnoses. By contrast, the fitter who diagnoses faults on the production line may have left school at 16 years of age and acquired a few more years' training, leading to a suitable qualification. Both the medical and mechanical diagnostician have access to knowledge about the structure and behaviour of their domain, as well as rules of thumb that can lead to short cuts in the diagnostic process. However, we have found that the fitter has a less sophisticated process of reasoning, taking less account of the role of uncertainty and probability, preferring to deal in black and white answers. This can make the process of knowledge representation easier, because of the straightforward reasoning process used by the experts.

By contrast, the knowledge acquisition process may be more difficult if the experts are unpractised in articulating what they do. This may not be due to lack of ability, but may be due to the behaviour having become so habitual that the expert has forgotten the original justification for the action. Over-learned behaviour of this kind can be difficult to justify within an expert system, because if there is no good reason for believing the behaviour, there may be no good reason for believing that the expert system recommends the correct behaviour.

Two kinds of knowledge are presented to the KBS builder. One is the heuristic, experiential kind of knowledge of the expert of many years' standing. The other is the theoretical knowledge of the trainee, who knows all the theory but not the details of practice. The designer of the system may be able to tell how the system should work, but might have to think quite hard to predict how it would go wrong. The expert fitter knows how the thing ought to work too, but can tell exactly the many ways in which it goes wrong.

Knowledge acquisition is the process of acquiring knowledge with which to construct a knowledge-based system, and data acquisition is the continuing activity of acquiring input data so that the KBS may provide advice. The medical diagnostician acquires data by examining and asking questions of the patient or by assessing the results of tests and monitors. In the medical case, much of the data may be fairly subjective in nature, relying perhaps on the patient's descriptions of sensations. By contrast, the industrial control system may be based on objective data, acquired through sensors. The human expert acquires much of his data unconsciously, perhaps by touch or smell, and might not even be aware of having acquired the data. The use of sensors can offer reliable sources of data, over an extended period of time.

Unfortunately, sensors are not always reliable – they develop calibration errors, break down or might not be able to measure the required ranges of parameters. This will be discussed further in Chapter 3, but for the moment we point out that good sensors are crucial to the development of knowledge-based systems for industrial control. Without direct sensor input, the speed of response of the system is limited by the keyboard input, with a user who might not be familiar with the design or layout of the keys. If historical data are not available to the system, complex fault scenarios are difficult to identify. In domains where time is important, the speed of data acquisition is an important factor in the speed of fault identification and correction. On-line control and fault detection depend on good sensor input.

The last reason for focussing on industrial control for the development of knowledge-based systems is that they can provide quite quickly a satisfactory return on investment. There are sound economic reasons for desiring to minimise plant downtime due to faults, achieving the best quality control and improving the safety of the plant's operation. Greater complexity of plant may be necessary for good return on investment, but this may be lost if the plant becomes too complex for humans to control it effectively.

Computer systems must be brought in, therefore, to cope. The initial investment required to set up a fault diagnosis system may be a few thousand pounds or less. More sophisticated systems take longer to develop and may require expensive hardware and longer commissioning periods, requiring investment of tens or hundreds of thousands of pounds. We suggest methods in Chapter 10 for reducing some of the costs.

In this section, we have reviewed the features of industrial control that make it distinct from the areas traditionally associated with knowledge-based systems. The main points are that the domains and their environments are or may be bounded, with a controllable amount of complexity. Time is important because the state of the plant may be changed during or by the process of consultation. The skills of the experts are accessible, provided industrial relations problems can be avoided. Automatic data acquisition, providing historical records, improves the speed of accuracy or performance, leading to an adequate return on the investment involved.

2.7 Tasks of industrial control

The lowest level of control consists of managing a process which takes material inputs, applies some change to them and endeavours to maintain the process output within specified limits around a setpoint. Minor fluctuations in the operating environment or quality of the inputs may be coped with by the controller, which will take corrective action so as to restore the process output to the setpoint. Typically, control actions at this level may be needed as often as every few milliseconds or only once an hour.

When the plant disturbances are more drastic or a fault develops, the controller cannot cope. The plant operator may summon assistance or an automatically monitored system may indicate an alarm. At this stage a different kind of expertise may be involved. The experienced diagnostician would observe the state of the plant and make a few guesses about what could have gone wrong. Some faults may be more common than others, so it would be sensible to check them first. A few extra tests may be required to identify exactly the fault or faults.

In order to carry out the diagnostic task, the expert might need to look at other pieces of equipment located physically near to the source of the alarm or which may be responsible for supplying its input or drawing off the output. Whereas low-level process control requires little more than the awareness of a single vessel and its associated sensors, fault diagnosis requires knowledge of the interconnected pieces of plant. The time-scale of fault occurrence could typically range from a fault developing on a particular piece of equipment about once every hour to once a year or more. A fitter might diagnose and repair a dozen faults or so a day.

In selecting tests to distinguish between candidate faults, the fitter needs to know more than just which machines are associated with each other, but also how they behave. For example, adjusting a valve setting at one point should be indicated by a change in a sensor and an alteration in the appearance of material x there. Given knowledge of interconnections and behaviours, it is a short step to reconfiguring the plant to avoid or cure faults. For example, if a blockage is building up in a pipe, then increasing the input pressure could clear the blockage. Alternatively, knowing the alternative pathways through the plant means that the faulty piece of piping could be avoided and shut off for replacement. Realistically, the fitter might not have responsibility for altering the state of the plant in this way, but his suggestion could be implemented by a plant scheduler.

Scheduling is the activity of allocating tasks to different components within the plant. For example, a paint shop could have many different paint sprayers, with a set of car bodies to paint in different colours, but minimising the number of changes of paint colour for each sprayer. Formal techniques exist for drawing up optimised schedules, but these need to be adapted quickly by the scheduler in response to equipment breaking down, staff falling sick or urgent jobs coming in.

The scheduling activity also requires knowledge about the interconnections between plant components, and historical data about the frequency of breakdown and length of down-time would also be useful. Scheduling is often done once a week, but adjustments to the schedule may be required several times a day.

The next highest level of activity is planning, occurring at the longest time-scale. Again, the time-scale can vary enormously, but would typically be monthly to once every few years, depending on the complexity of the system being managed. Planning is another activity that has received plenty of attention within AI. An important approach to planning proceeds by formulating an overall plan and refining each step to ever greater levels of detail. Ultimately, the plans could come down to the level of schedules.

Planning means making long-term decision about the role of the plant in a wider context, within the external environment of the local economy and markets. Decisions will not only be about the quantity of different products to manufacture, but will also concern the fabric of the plant itself, such as the necessity to shut down, re-open or extend parts of the plant. In these circumstances, skilled designers may be needed who can design a plant to fulfil certain production requirements, but paying attention to costs, reliability and safety. Many possible designs could be conceived, but their flexibility for scheduling, reliability for maintenance and ease of process control all need to be considered (*see* Table 2.1).

Table 2.1 The range of activities covered by industrial process control

Activity	Time-scale	Kinds of knowledge	Kinds of inference	Linked on
Low-level control	milliseconds to hours	Process	Forward chaining	
				Alarm monitoring
Fault diagnosis	hours to years	Process and plant	Forward chaining Backward chaining Qualitative simulation Hypothesis list management Test generation	
				Plant re-configuration
Scheduling	weekly	Plant	Constraint matching Constraint specification Schedule generation Schedule critiquing Justification	
				Refinement of plans
Planning – design	years	Process and plant	Simulation Critiquing Parts list generation Risk assessment	
– economic	years	Process (external world)	Simulation What-if scenario generation Critiquing Plan refinement	
Training		Process plant	Critiquer Explainer all of the above	

2.8 Expert systems for low-level control and fault diagnosis

The previous section presented an overview of the tasks of industrial control, and earlier in the chapter, a short indication was made of the different styles of interaction possible with expert systems. This sets the scene for the remainder of the book.

For now, we shall concentrate on expert systems for low-level control and fault diagnosis. Table 2.1 shows that these are not the only kinds of expert systems possible, but they have already been quite widely implemented in industry and a body of experience is beginning to emerge.

Expert systems for low-level control and fault diagnosis differ significantly from systems for scheduling and planning. In control and diagnosis, there is a limited number of conclusions which the expert system could reach. There are only so many control actions that may be taken, and there are only so many things that can go wrong with a piece of equipment. Hence, these systems can be thought of as *classificatory*, ie they examine the state of the world and classify it into one of a limited set of states. Planning and scheduling are much more open-ended problems. Potentially, an unlimited range of options is possible, but constraints exist to keep the number to a manageable level. Planning and scheduling are *synthesising* problems, in that the outcome of the systems will be a newly synthesised plan or schedule and not an assignment to a pre-existing classification.

This affects the inference style of the two kinds of problem. Low-level control and fault diagnosis can rely upon forward and backward chaining to infer from data to conclusions, but scheduling and planning use search to explore the large space of possible solutions. This difference is reflected in Table 2.1.

The distinction between classification and search expert systems is fairly simply made. However, it is not strictly true that all problems in fault diagnosis can be solved by inference alone, nor are all problems in scheduling strictly search. Mixtures of inference methods can be used in complex KBS, but the distinction is worth noting. For the remainder of this book, we shall be concentrating on classification expert systems and shall not be exploring further the use of search within industrial control. Our attention will be focussed on low-level control and fault diagnosis as examples of problems that can be solved using forward and backwards chaining.

As explained above, low-level control and fault diagnosis differ from scheduling and planning, but they also differ markedly from each other.

Expert systems for low-level control would be expected to operate continuously and automatically, with the human controller maintaining supervision over the system. A fault diagnosis expert system would be used under consultation, where a fitter wants advice on how to repair a fault. The low-level control expert system operates continuously, whereas the fault diagnosis system operates only as requested.

The low-level controller would acquire its data through sensors, but the fault diagnoser might rely on a mixture of sensor and keyboard input from the fitter. The controller would be expected to operate in real-time, matching its speed of execution with that of the process. The fault diagnoser would also need to be as quick as possible. In particular, if an emergency is likely to occur, its response should not be overtaken by the speed at which faults develop.

An expert system for low-level process control, we shall assume, will operate without direct intervention from the process operator. The expert system exercises its control function just as any other kind of automatic controller. Its performance is likely to be under the supervision of a skilled process operator. The fault diagnosis expert system is more likely to be used as an advisor to the skilled repairman, suggesting possible diagnoses and recommending a repair procedure. The fault diagnoser would have no direct access to the faulty component, so relies upon the fitter to execute its recommendations. The fault diagnoser would be an advisory system, but the controller would be supervised.

2.9 Concluding remarks

Expert systems are another technological advance which may be used to improve the performance of industry. Their historical development has concentrated on their use in other fields, so this chapter is an attempt to leave all that behind. The requirements of expert systems in industrial control are quite different, so we need to examine what the differences are between industrial use and other uses. Moreover, an expert system approach to industrial control is very different from the usual mathematical approach, so it is also important to look at the problems of industry from an AI perspective.

This chapter sets out to adjust the reader's perspective to the remainder of the book. Some simplifications have been made in the interests of clarity, but this is an active research area, so many advances are likely to be seen in the next five to ten years. However, the basic ideas have already shown their merit in application and are likely to go on yielding dividends for a long time to come.

Chapter 3 Knowledge representation

3.1 Introduction

The knowledge representation format most often associated with expert systems is the If . . . Then rule. This chapter will discuss the application of rules, and how they have been extended to cope with uncertainty. Some of the problems associated with the use of rules will be discussed and this will show why other formats, such as the frame, have developed. Logic and neural nets as means of representing knowledge will also be discussed.

3.2 What knowledge representation does

An expert system uses knowledge to solve problems within a limited domain of expertise. Somehow, that knowledge has to be stored within the computer for manipulation by programs that carry out inference and other tasks. The knowledge will be culled from the world in a hotch-potch of different forms and from a variety of sources. This all has to be formalised and structured in some way, so that it will be usable by the machine, but may be shown to the user in an understandable form.

Within science fiction, the ultimate goal of artificial intelligence might appear to be to construct a mechanical brain, a machine with all the knowledge and reasoning power of a human, capable of understanding and expressing emotion but with powers beyond ours. Expert systems are much more modest in their aims. The simplest expert systems are strictly limited in the domains of knowledge which they deal with and are capable only of very rudimentary reasoning. Their abilities to represent knowledge are very restricted. Their advantages and usefulness stem from their large and reliable memories and ability to perform consistently.

Given that artificial brains are not yet with us, we must realise that the knowledge that may be stored within an expert system is limited, not only by the memory capacity of the computer, but also by the knowledge representation format that it uses. Some kinds of knowledge are better suited to one representation than another, in that the representation is more efficient in terms of symbols used and in its intelligibility to the human who is encoding the knowledge within that representation. For example, imagine the London Underground map. The map is a source of information, allowing users easily to plan a route around London from one station to any other. The same information could be presented as a table or a huge collection of If . . . Then rules. However, it would be much harder to use and, in the absence of the familiar visual image of the map, constructing and comparing alternative routes would be impossible without the help of pencil and paper.

The choice of knowledge representation format is important, since it will determine, to some extent, the kinds of knowledge that the expert system can hold. Some kinds of knowledge can be easily and quickly represented by rules, but if other kinds of knowledge start to become important during the life-time of the expert system, then it might be better to introduce new knowledge representation formats, rather than force knowledge into an existing, inappropriate format. However, If . . . Then rules are very suitable to applications in process control, as we shall see throughout the remainder of this book.

The choice of knowledge representation format cannot be made without some understanding of the kinds of conclusions that are required of the expert system. The expert system builder must ensure that these conclusions may be drawn from knowledge represented in the chosen way, and that they may be drawn efficiently. It might be better not to represent all the knowledge available if another, more restricted representation enables crucial decisions to be made quickly.

Furthermore, the knowledge still needs to be translated into the format by a knowledge engineer, so the format should be understandable, or be supported by tools (usually software) that make it usable.

If an expert system performs its job well, it might be tempting for users who are not perhaps fully aware of how it works to believe that the expert system actually has some understanding of how the process works, how the equipment is interconnected and what the rules really mean. This is, of course, not so. An expert system manipulates symbols according to programs, without any interest or understanding of what the symbols mean. When the symbols are presented to the user of the expert system, he or she ascribes meaning to them.

3.3 If . . . Then rules

If . . . Then rules, as a formalism, are not a recent invention. They have been used in the psychology, automata theory and formal grammars. They have many names, such as production rules, situation-action rules, condition-action rules or just productions. The rules consist of an If-part and a Then-part:

If A_1 & A_2 . . . & A_n Then B_1 & B_2 . . . & B_m

The If-part, A_1 & A_2 . . . & A_n, is sometimes known as the premise, condition, antecedent or left-hand side. The Then-part, B_1 & B_2 . . . & B_m, is known as the conclusion, consequent, action or right-hand side.

The syntax of If . . . Then rules is straightforward enough, but we should think carefully about the semantics of such rules. A situation-action rule would be read as 'If situation A_1 & A_2 ... & A_n is true, then perform action B_1 & B_2 ... & B_m'. Thus, the right-hand side does not necessarily follow from the left-hand side. Some agent, whether a person or machine, must intervene to carry out the action. These rules are not as 'strong' in the connection from left-hand side to right-hand side as strictly logical rules of implication, where the right-hand side necessarily follows, in every possible world, which may be written as:

$$A_1 \text{ \& } A_2 \ldots \text{ \& } A_n \Rightarrow B_1 \text{ \& } B_2 \ldots \text{ \& } B_m$$

When the rules are understood as condition-action rules, the semantics are slightly different again. Here, the reading would be: 'If conditions A_1 & A_2 ... & A_n are true, then *conclude* that B_1 & B_2 ... & B_m are true.' This is similar to the situation-action rule, with the action being to conclude that something is true. It might be more realistic to take the action of a condition-action rule as 'believe that something is true' or merely 'suspect that something is true'. This is because in the messy, uncertain, real world, we would not often be happy to place all our bets on the outcome of one rule. There might be some hitherto unsuspected condition which should have been included in the left-hand side, which means that the conclusion cannot validly be drawn. Or the checking of the conditions might have been faulty or the state of the conditions might have changed since they were checked, or some other thing. One thing is clear, we rarely believe absolutely in practice in the conclusions of rules. How then can we cope with the problem of knowledge representation and inference under uncertainty?

3.4 Coping with uncertainty

A rule-based expert system is an example of a pattern-directed inference system, where incoming data are matched against the collection of rules and when a pattern of data matches the left-hand side of some rule or rules, they are fired and some action occurs. Chains of inference may be set up, as we shall see in the next chapter, but at the point of firing a rule, the truth of the rule's left-hand side is propagated to the right-hand side, which then becomes true too. So, at any time, we can decide which left-hand sides are true and which are false and 'mark' each one accordingly. Hence, each left-hand side has a 'truth bearing item', which may be examined to see if the associated statement is true or not.

Other rule-based knowledge representation formats extend their capacity to represent knowledge by associating other 'truth bearing items', such as a certainty factor, with the proposition, instead of or together with the simple truth value. *See* Table 3.1 for some examples.

The values of the truth bearing items are propagated during inference and at the end of the consultation, several conclusions

---

Table 3.1 Rules qualified with items to represent uncertainty
High-IOP is-a-cause-of-retinal-damage (.7)

Spots is-usually-a-symptom-of measles

RULE: 'calculate likelihood that control and
recovered samples are from the same origin'
same-origin DEPENDS ON
RI-evidence   AFFIRMS 70.0   DENIES −80.0
Elem-Anal-evidence   AFFIRMS 20.0   DENIES −40.0

---

may be presented for consideration, ordered with respect to the value of the truth bearing item. Therefore, if the truth bearing item is taken to mean 'likelihood', then the conclusion with the highest value may be understood as the most likely.

The knowledge representation formats of Table 3.1 try to represent the uncertainty associated with the propositions, by using a probability value to qualify the statement. The probabilities are intended to indicate the probability of the right-hand side being true when the left-side is true. These examples use only a single number to represent uncertainty and the propagation of these values is based on Bayes theorem.

$$\text{Bayes theorem} \quad \frac{P(H_i|E) = P(E|H_i) * P(H_i)}{\sum_{n=1}^{k} P(E|H_n) * P(H_n)}$$

There are a number of problems associated with single-valued truth bearing items, which apply to all Bayesian techniques.

All Bayesian techniques depend upon the global assumption of evidence independence. This requires that all the items of evidence that are used to support a hypothesis must have no correlations and no causal relationships. For example, suppose one wanted to establish whether it was raining. On looking out of the window, one could see that the street was wet. Further observation might show that raindrops were splashing in the puddles. These two pieces of evidence could not be used independently to support the belief that it was raining. Either one alone might provide some support, but their close causal connection would mean that the support they jointly provide would be less than that of two independent pieces of evidence. It would be an easy mistake to make to overlook this important effect when constructing or running an expert system.

Not only ought the evidence be mutually independent, the hypotheses too must obey some rigorous conditions. The hypotheses should exhaustively cover the entire space of possibility, which might mean constructing a catch-all hypothesis. The hypotheses should also be exclusive, meaning that no hypothesis should subsume any other. These conditions might not appear to be very difficult to meet in practice, given some careful thought, but one should wonder whether 'working' expert systems do indeed satisfy these constraints. If they do not, then their conclusions can have little value.

Should an expert system be constructed that obeys all the required conditions, it might still be difficult to understand the answers that are produced. The conclusions will be qualified by a single numerical value and it can be difficult to assign the value a sensible meaning. Often, the rank ordering of the numbers is all that is useful. Users of the expert system might have their own suspicions of the validity of the numbers that the machine produces, especially since they are often quoted to several decimal places of accuracy and the users know that the numerical values they supplied were very imprecise and inaccurate.

Such difficulties of input arise from the often ambiguous nature of the questions that the expert system asks, leaving the user unsure of what the system actually wants. For example, the question: *How certain are you that you suffer from stress?* is sometimes interpreted as being the same as: *How much stress do you suffer from?*

Clearly, these questions address two similar but different problems. People would expect to be asked questions more like the second of the two above and so are likely to answer the first question as if it were the second. Such user behaviour is quite understandable, but it would compromise the validity of the numerical results. Rather than criticise the users and builders of the expert system, we should acknowledge instead that the knowledge representation is inadequate and inappropriate.

Two numerical values

Some of the difficulties of Bayesian reasoning may be avoided by using two numbers to represent an extra degree of uncertainty. One might not know for certain that a probability has the exact value 0.7, but would feel more comfortable saying that it lies somewhere between 0.5 and 0.9.

Under conditions of complete ignorance about the truth value of a proposition A, Bayesian reasoning requires that $p(A)$ and $p(-A)$ should sum to unity, so one is obliged to say that they are both equal to 0.5, even though remaining in complete ignorance of their actual values, which could lie anywhere between 0 and 1. Suppose the proposition A was 'When I toss this coin it will land heads up', it would be possible to carry out experiments to measure the proportion of times that the coin actually does fall heads up. At the end of the experiment, one might be able to say that the coin is fair and that the probability if A is indeed as exactly equal to 0.5 as the experiment would permit. Bayesian reasoning gives no means of representing the reduction in uncertainty that these experiments have provided. Some means of representing ignorance is required.

Shafer-Dempster Theory allows the representation of ignorance, so that $p(A) + p(-A) \leqslant 1$. One may state upper and lower bounds on the values of the probability of some proposition being true.

Also, Shafer-Dempster permits the distribution of a probability 'mass' over a set of propositions. For example, suppose an analysis was being done of the future sales of five car manufacturers, Toyota, Daihatsu, Fiat, Rover Group and Renault. *See* Table 3.2.

Shafer-Dempster allows probability to be assigned to the propositions of Table 3.2, whereas Bayesian reasoning would require a probability to be assigned to the proposition for each single car manufacturer, with joint and conditional probabilities to be worked out to cover the propositions of Table 3.2.

Table 3.2 Car sales.
  {Toyota, Daihatsu, Fiat, Rover Group, Renault)
  p (Japanese cars will dominate the market)
  p (European cars will dominate the market)
  p (Rover Group will dominate the market)

The Shafer-Dempster theory of evidence has some strong points. It allows the explicit statement of the evidence supporting and denying a hypothesis. Uncertainty may be represented as the gap between the probabilities of an event occurring and not occurring.

Data are represented at an appropriate level of granularity. Thus, if all we have data about is the probability of Japanese cars dominating the market, then we may represent the data as exactly that, rather than having to assign that probability mass over separate hypotheses concerning each of the Japanese manufacturers.

On the down side, Shafer-Dempster theory relies on the same global assumptions as Bayes theorem. The inference procedures do not retain any record of how each individual piece of evidence affected the overall conclusion, so tracing the aggregation and propagation of beliefs and evidence is not straightforward.

A vector of numerical values

Instead of relying on only a pair of values to represent uncertainty, some methods use a vector of values, such as Fuzzy Reasoning.

Fuzzy Reasoning is based on Fuzzy Set Theory, which we shall return to in Chapter 7. A fuzzy set is used to represent the linguistic concepts that are frequently used by humans when they describe the world. These terms may be vague and are not readily represented by the kinds of propositions that predicate logic deals with. For example, temperature adjectives, such as 'warm', 'cool' and 'hot' are impossible to define crisply, with a temperature above which something is described as warm and below which it is not described as warm. Fuzzy reasoning gets around this by dispensing with the zero or one grades of membership, where an item is a member of a set or it is not, and admitting grades of membership, anywhere in the range between and including zero and one (*see* Figure 3.1).

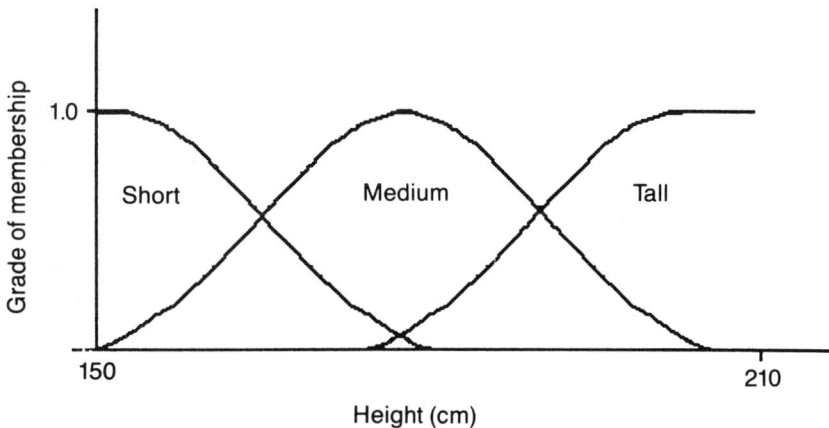

Figure 3.1 Some fuzzy sets to describe the height of tall men

These linguistic terms may be manipulated using the usual connectives of 'and', 'or' and 'but', but with the addition of others, such as 'very' and 'rather'. So, a newspaper headline like 'Big San Francisco quake unlikely for a while, experts say' would be represented, using traditional probability, as something like:

$$p \text{ (magnitude} \leqslant 7, 0 \leqslant \text{Occurrence} \leqslant 10) \leqslant 0.1 \qquad (3.1)$$

meaning that the probability of an earthquake of magnitude on the Richter scale greater than 7 occurring within the next ten years is less or equal to 0.1. A fuzzy representation would be:

$$p \text{ (Strength is HIGH, Occurrence is SOON)} = \text{unlikely.} \qquad (3.2)$$

The fuzzy representation retains the original linguistic phrases, making it easier for a reader to understand, but more complex to represent numerically.

Fuzzy reasoning does not depend on any assumptions of global evidence independence or on the exhaustiveness and exclusiveness of hypotheses. Evidence is accumulated and represented as it is available, in a fairly undisciplined manner.

Again, it is difficult to disentangle the reasons for supporting or refuting a hypothesis at the end of a consultation. And the aggregation and propagation of uncertainty are untraceable.

Other methods for handling uncertainty

Numerical methods for coping with uncertainty come in many varieties. The probabilistic methods have a sound mathematical foundation, but are difficult to apply properly in practice. Other ad hoc methods have been devised, as in MYCIN, but these can lead to unexpected results. The final numerical value provided by these techniques can be difficult to interpret, particularly since it might be the result of all sorts of uncertain notions during the consultation.

Other methods are being suggested now, such as logics designed specifically to reason *about* uncertainty, rather than trying to propagate an 'uncertainty-bearing item' during the inference process. Adding extensions to existing logics doesn't seem to have been successful, so people are trying to devise new logics for exactly the purpose required.

3.5 Rule-based knowledge representation in process control

Many criticisms have been levelled against rules, but these do not always apply in the domain of low-level process control and fault diagnosis. In this section, we shall look at the particular qualities of these domains and how they affect the use of rules. *See* Table 3.3 for a summary of the criticisms which will be discussed.

Table 3.3 Summary of criticisms made of rule-based knowledge representation
- new rules may interfere unpredictably with rules already in the knowledge base
- rules that are easy to read and good for generating explanations are inefficient to execute
- rules are not good for representing the richness and complexity of knowledge

One of the often quoted advantages of expert systems was the alleged ability to add more and more rules to the knowledge base, so-called incremental knowledge acquisition. This belief has been shaken lately because it is not necessarily true. Even in logic programs the order in which rules occur in the knowledge base can affect the conclusions that are reached. However, this criticism is less important in the domains of both low-level control and industrial fault diagnosis than might at first appear.

The reason this criticism is so important is because many domains lack structure and are very complex, with many parameters and variables. The decision space is potentially very large and fraught with complex interrelationships. A process which is controlled by a human expert is described in terms of a handful of variables, with perhaps their derivatives and integrals. Hence, the decision space is well-bounded. The left-hand side of each rule will have a particular set of clauses, and it is straightforward to check which clauses need to be included. The range of values each variable can take may also be specified in advance, which ensures two things, that each new rule may be checked to see if it overlaps with any already present and that the knowledge base may be checked for completeness, so that no areas of the decision space are uncovered. It is possible that the left-hand sides of the rules could become awkwardly long and complex, but if this looks like happening, then it is worth trying to structure the rules more or split them up into blocks, according to the value of critical variables for example.

Turning to fault diagnosis, we must also beware of new rules interfering with the old. Again, this problem is best anticipated by structuring the rule-base so that the possibility of undetected interference is prevented as far as possible. Fortunately, the domain of industrial fault diagnosis lends itself well to structuring, because the rules for an individual component, type of component or part of the process can be readily grouped together. Structuring the knowledge base in this way has the added advantage of improving the speed at which the expert system executes. Furthermore, many commercially useful expert systems contain a surprisingly small number of rules, 100 or less, so that maintaining the knowledge base need not be so complex.

Any medium of communication between people and computers meets with difficulties. In the early days of computing, assembler was criticised because it was less efficient in terms of machine time than the beloved machine code, although it was easier for programmers to use. Languages that are easy for people to use have a trade-off on computer storage and execution speed. There are a number of reasons why process control need not be overly worried by this line of thinking.

In low-level control, the operator does not rely upon the expert system to generate explanations from its rules, although this is possible when required. Instead, the operator is receiving information from many different sources and once the expert system has been installed and accepted, the operator is likely to want explanations very rarely. Also, it is quite possible to have two forms of the rules, one representation to achieve speed of execution and another to be used to generate explanations. This solution could also be used for fault diagnosis, where both speed of execution and intelligible explanations are required.

Rules are a fairly crude tool for representing knowledge. They are superficial and shallow. They are not good for representing notions of time, causality and intent. So we should design rule-based expert systems with these limitations in mind. Any engineer knows to select the right tools for the job. If the job demands an expert system that can monitor a plant, detect and diagnose errors, recommend a safe shutdown, suggest the most efficient repair procedure and enable a safe and speedy start-up, then rules are not the thing to use. But, for a reliable low-level controller or ready assistant on fault diagnosis, then rules are up to the task.

The tasks of low-level control and fault diagnosis have already been presented as classifactory tasks, ie selecting one from a set of possible classifications based on information about the state of the world. Classification, within a limited domain is a task that can be carried out by rule-based systems. If the goal of the system designer changes, so that fault diagnosis should be accompanied by generated repair procedures etc, then the task is no longer classification, but synthesis. At that point, other knowledge, with the appropriate representation, will be required.

3.6 Structured knowledge representations

Any Artificial Intelligence program attempts, at some level, to emulate the behaviour of a human. Debate rages over the extent to which the knowledge the program uses need resemble the knowledge a human would use. Rules might not be a good representation of the way the human brain stores knowledge on how to control processes, but at least they are a reasonable way to represent the way a human would *describe* how to control a process. The extensions to the basic rule-based format discussed earlier do not take as their motivation the desire to model what goes on in the human mind. Rather, they try to make the computer use representations more appropriate to its hardware (viz numbers) to produce behaviour similar to that of a human. Other knowledge representation formats have tried to improve the performance of artificial intelligence programs by using knowledge representation formats that are more 'natural', in that they might have more similarities with the way the human brain stores knowledge. This section and the final section of this chapter will discuss such formats.

There are three important basic structured formats for representing knowledge, the graph, the frame and the object.

Graphs

The kinds of graphs to be considered here are the formal, mathematical kind and not plots of one variable against another. A graph consists of a collection of *nodes*, which may be joined together by *links*. The nodes are usually labelled and the links might be labelled too, if there is more than one kind of link.

A special kind of graph is the tree, where the links are directed, and there are no loops within the graph. Trees are often used to represent classifications, with the links being known as is-a or is-part links (*see* Figure 3.2(a) and (b)).

Some graphs allow loops so as to construct networks, perhaps with many different kinds of link between nodes (*see* Figure 3.3). This kind of graph is called a 'semantic net' because they were first used to try to represent concepts in natural language.

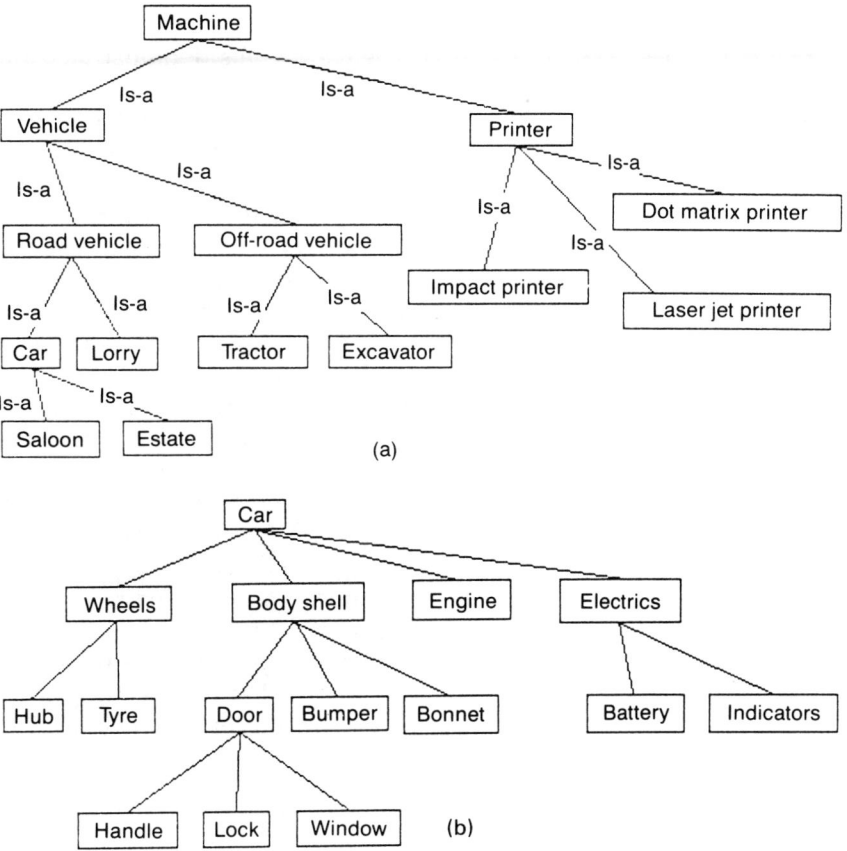

Figure 3.2 (a) Is-a and (b) Is-part hierarchies

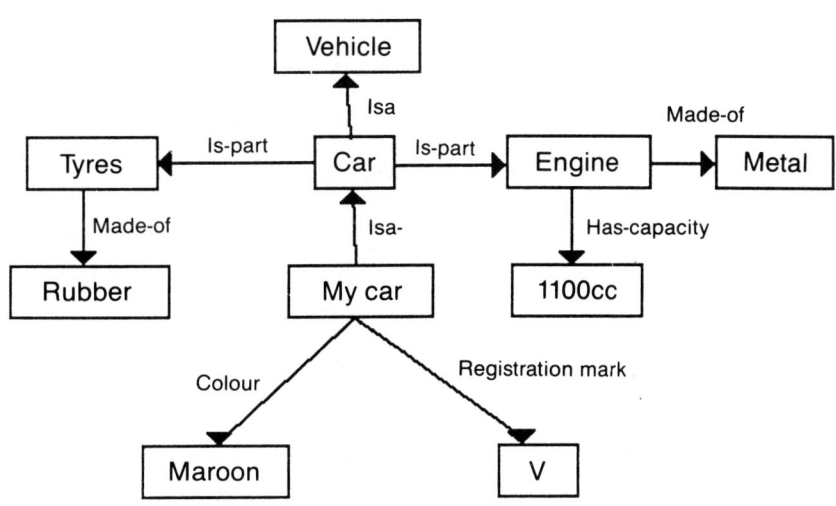

Figure 3.3 A semantic net

Frames

Semantic nets demonstrated that there are many connections between concepts as represented in the human mind. But the kind of hierarchical representation of the graph is also important. Frames capture the hierarchical nature of much commonsense knowledge, and also the intuition that we have a cluster of ideas associated with each concept.

Frames are used to group information, like in a record in a database. Each record has a collection of 'slots', which are filled with data. The frames may form a hierarchy, so slots may be filled by inheriting values from the parent in the hierarchy. This mechanism can be used to represent assumptions and defaults which we believe to be true about the world. The defaults can be overridden with values that pertain to a particular example from a class. So, we could represent knowledge about the general class of animals, then about the class of birds, then about canaries and finally about a particular instance or example of a canary, viz Tweety (*see* Figure 3.4).

Frames may be used to represent many of the assumptions of everyday, commonsense reasoning. Set theory provides mathematical structures which are well-defined and elegant, but are not good at representing human knowledge. Frames do not follow the notions of sets and subsets, but something more like

Animal
Is-a: Living-thing
Has-legs: (2, 4, 6, 8, more)
Lives-in: (Hole, Nest, Den)
Has-colour: Default: Brown

Bird
Is-a: Animal
Has-legs: 2
Lives-in: Nest
Has-colour: Default: Brown
Flies: (Yes, No)
Wing-span: unknown
Migratory: (Yes, No)

Canary
Is-a: Bird
Has-colour: Yellow
Flies: Yes
Wing-span: 20 cm approx

Tweety
Is-a: Canary
Lives-in: Cage
Enemy: Sylvester

Figure 3.4 A hierarchy of frames

general classes, with specialisations, examples, instances and exceptions. (Fuzzy set theory takes a different approach to relaxing the axioms of set theory; *see* Chapter 7.) There is some psychological evidence to support the belief that frames are analogous in some ways to human memory.

Objects

Frames were first suggested in 1975 and saw favour for about ten years. Since then, we have recently seen the rise of object-oriented systems. Whereas frames concentrated on the inheritance of data from a general class to a more specialised instance of that class, object-oriented systems enable the inheritance of procedures as well as data.

An object consists of a collection of data items, some of which may have been defined as particular to that object and others inherited from higher up the hierarchy. Various procedures may be applied to that object, such as '+' or 'place-in-ascending-order', with the object deciding how to interpret that procedure. For example, a real number would understand '+' as meaning 'take the sum of myself and the next parameter(s)'; a string might carry out a procedure to concatenate itself with the next parameter(s); a triangle might have a specially defined procedure which takes '+' to mean 'enlarge myself by the fixed amount and draw myself on the screen'.

Object-oriented systems are becoming popular now because they are good at supporting program development by prototyping. The first useful object-oriented system was Smalltalk, which also benefited from the now familiar 'WIMP' screen display, with windows, icons, a mouse and pointers. Such user interfaces are now becoming commonplace, since the advent of the Apple Lisa and Macintosh. Object-oriented programming is available under Lisp and as derivatives of procedural languages. Lisp forms the basis for Loops, KEE, Flavors and others. Actor and C++ are object-oriented languages with a syntax more familiar to non-Lisp programmers.

Mixed representations

Many knowledge representation formats are used because knowledge comes in many shapes and forms. A single representation will not be adequate to represent all the knowledge available, nor will it support the other requirements which have to do with speed of execution and memory requirements. Mixed representations are finding favour, therefore.

Hierarchies of frames or objects have been used to model the general concepts of components in a factory, with increasing specialisation the further down the hierarchy (*see* Figure 3.5).

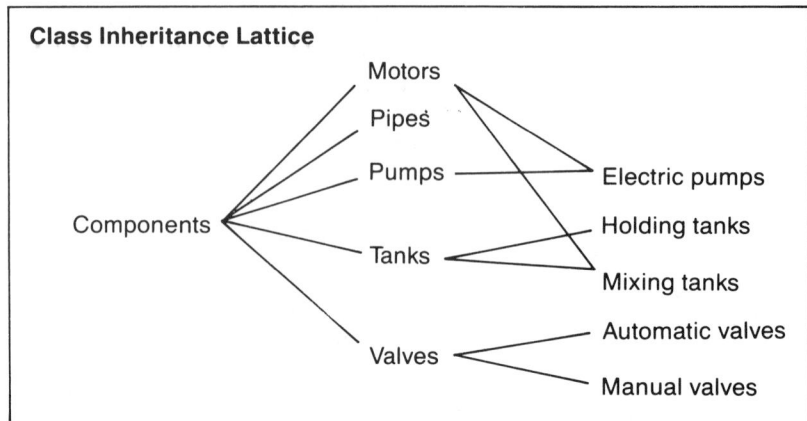

Class Inheritance Lattice

Motors
Pipes
Pumps ——————— Electric pumps
Components
Holding tanks
Tanks
Mixing tanks
Automatic valves
Valves
Manual valves

Figure 3.5 A hierarchy of classes for factory components (from Koukoulis)

Combined with the frames are small, local rule-bases with details of fault-finding or low-level control knowledge. It is likely that this is the way that production and process control will go in the future as more and more intelligence is distributed to the components and sensors in the factory. The knowledge and operational requirements will drive different sorts of knowledge to different locations on-board the plant, so the supervisory system will have to be able to handle many kinds of knowledge and data from different sources.

However, although using mixed knowledge representations can lead to more expressiveness, it can also lead to more bugs, which are subtler and harder to track down. Mixed representations are good, but they require an experienced programmer, who knows what's going on and understands well the different representations and how they relate to each other.

3.7 Using logic to represent knowledge

The previous section discussed some recent developments in knowledge representation which follow a paradigm of using computer and software power to support representation formats which model human reasoning techniques. Cognitive psychology would give evidence to confirm these formats as analogous to the human mind, at some level. However, these techniques require skill to use and the complex software runs on expensive machines, with many facilities to enable the programmer to perform the task.

By contrast, the logic-based paradigm takes a quite different approach. Instead of supporting complex software, logic seeks to establish a compact and elegant framework of logical axioms, which provide a set of primitive terms within which to represent knowledge. The mathematical basis of logic means that the conclusions drawn would have high credibility, since they are stated within a formally correct and provable framework. Every conclusion would have the status of a theorem within the logic. So, contrary to popular opinion, logic did not finish with Aristotle.

In the rest of this section, we shall give a short introduction to some of the recent work in logic.

Predicate logic

Predicate logic represents facts about the world using predicates. For example, the fact:

Socrates is a man.

may be represented as:

Man (Socrates)

where *Man(.)* is the predicate and *Socrates* is the subject of the predicate. Facts about all men may be represented using qualified statements. The classic proposition:

All men are mortal

may be represented via the two predicates *Man(x)* and *Mortal(x)*:

$\forall x, man(x) \Rightarrow Mortal(x)$

The symbol, $\forall$, is the universal qualifier, usually read as 'for all'. The predicate logic formula above would be read as: For all x, if x is a man, then x is mortal.

Apart from the universal qualifier, there is also the existential qualifier $\exists$. Using this, the fact:

Everyone loves somebody

could be represented as:

$\forall x \exists y: loves\ (x,y)$

This formula would be read as: For all x, there exists a y so that x loves y. Note that *loves* takes two arguments, x and y, and is a two-place predicate.

Predicate logic is an intellectually appealing way to represent facts, since it has a well defined structure and elegant representation and inference methods. However, the facts that may be represented would appear stilted if this were all that could be known about life. Sentences taken from a novel or textbook would be very difficult to represent as formulae in predicate logic. However, for simpler worlds, predicate logic or something similar may well be useful for representing pertinent knowledge.

Rich provides a list of sentences that could not be represented using predicate logic, *see* Table 3.4.

Various logics have, however, been proposed to cope with statements like these. Modal logic is an extension of classical logic to deal initially with possibility and necessity. Current research

C

Table 3.4 Some sentences to defeat predicate logic

It is very hot today.
Blond-haired people often have blue eyes.
If there is no evidence to the contrary, assume that any adult you meet knows
   how to read.
It's better to have more pieces on the board than the opponent has.
I know Bill thinks the Giants will win, but I think they are going to lose.

---

uses modal logic to provide a framework for the analysis of belief, knowledge, obligation, time etc.

Modal logic

Modal logic uses the notation of ordinary logic supplemented with the box □, which is usually read as 'it is necessary that . . .'. So,

$$\Box A$$

is read as 'it is necessary that A (is true)'. Similarly,

$$\Box \neg A$$

is read as 'it is necessary that A is not true'. Compare this with

$$\neg \Box \neg A$$

which is read as 'it is possible that A is true', if you think about it hard enough.

Modal logic can be developed into a logic for reasoning about knowledge and belief, where □ is taken as meaning 'I know that'. Various interesting results about knowledge and awareness can be proven within this logic, such as:

$$\Box A \rightarrow \Box \, \Box A$$

which expresses a kind of introspection 'I know A, then I know that I know A.' This may be generalised to 'I know that I know.'

3.8 Neural nets

Neural nets are currently receiving attention as the next stage in knowledge representation. Rules, frames and objects represent attempts to model the human mind in some way. But, they are constructed as a result of people having to think or talk about how it is they do or understand things. Most of the time, we act apparently without thinking, knowing how to ride a bicycle, control a process or diagnose a disease without having to search for the right rule or piece of knowledge. Rules are an artefact of having to talk about knowledge. Psychology would argue that knowledge is not located in specific areas of the brain, but is stored within the network of the brain. Neural nets try to model the physical structure of the brain, using the interconnectedness of the net to represent knowledge.

A neural net consists of an array of elements (neurones), interconnections between the neurones and an input/output scheme. The interconnections between neurones, or the topology of the network, could have each neurone connected to only a few other neurones, to many neurones or to all the neurones in the network (*see* Figure 3.6).

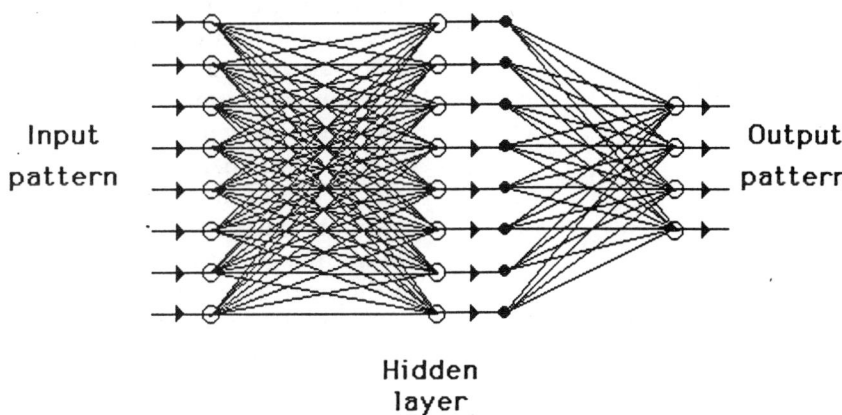

Figure 3.6 A simple neural net, with one hidden layer

Hidden layer

Patterns of input data are presented to the net, which uses a weighting scheme to pass signals to other nodes. A hidden layer or layers, intermediate between input and output nodes, may be used.

The neurones have learning rules to describe how each neurone interprets the information coming to it from all its connections and how it decides what signal to distribute to the rest of the network. There are many different rules, based on various factors, such as previous state of the neurone, fixed or varying thresholds and the functions used to sum the incoming signals.

Neural nets can be used in many different ways. The 'associative memory' form can be used for simple image recognition tasks, classifying arrays of pixels, with the help of a teacher to designate when the net is established how sample patterns should be classified. Neural nets may also be used to produce solutions to optimisation problems, such as the travelling salesman problem. For N locations on a map, the travelling salesman must pick the shortest route between the locations, visiting each one once. There are $N!$ possible paths and this number gets very large very quickly. A neural net can find a near-optimal solution very quickly, which is often better than finding the optimal solution slowly. Self-organising neural nets could be used to learn to approximate a mapping for a robot control strategy based only on randomly sampled inputs from a two-dimensional space.

Single processor, serial programming is beginning to reach its limits. Programmers are having trouble keeping up with the demand for software. A computing device that exploits the possibilities of parallel computing *and* can teach itself how to perform is bound to be worth investigating.

3.9 Concluding remarks

Knowledge representation is a fascinating topic, with many formats being suggested to represent parts of the knowledge and skills of the human brain. Expert systems can be constructed using very simple knowledge representation schemes, but the designers and users of such systems soon begin to think of ways to improve on their early attempts.

Knowledge representation schemes can take their inspiration from the organisation and complexity of the human brain or they can try to improve their performance by producing formal and rigorous schemes. Both approaches have been discussed above. Neural nets offer another exciting approach likely to show promise in the next ten years.

The goal of research on knowledge representation is to improve the performance of expert systems by giving them a better understanding of the domain in which they operate.

Chapter 4 Inference

4.1 Introduction

The previous chapter discussed how rules can be used to represent knowledge and examined some other knowledge representation formats. This chapter will describe the kinds of inference that may be carried out with rules, and how these and other techniques may be useful in industrial control.

4.2 Inference with rules

There are three basic components to a rule-based expert system, apart from the programs (*see* Figure 4.1)

- the rule base;
- working memory;
- a control strategy.

The rule-base contains a collection of rules, pertinent to the problems that the expert system is to address. Some of the rules might be of a fairly general nature, but others might be very specific to the particular domain.

The working memory stores data and facts. The expert system acquires data from the outside world, which is represented in the working memory. As the expert system examines the data and the

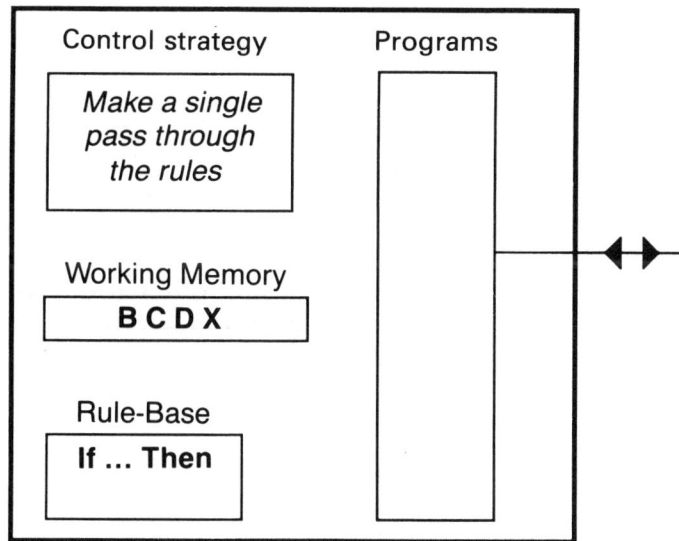

Figure 4.1 Components of a rule-based expert system

rule-base, other facts and hypotheses may be derived and placed in the working memory. At the point of storing the facts in working memory, they may be tagged with other information, such as their source, time of creation etc.

The control strategy controls the application of the rules to the data. Various strategies are possible, controlling on the number of times each rule is applied, how the rules are compared cyclically etc.

There are two main techniques for carrying out inference with rules: forward and backward chaining. The easiest way to explain them and to convey the role of each of the above components is with the help of some examples.

4.3 Forward chaining

A few simple rules are presented in Table 4.1, which will be used to illustrate the discussion that follows.

The rules may be read as 'If A then X', 'If B then Y' in the first two cases. For these two rules, A and B are the antecedents and X and Y are the consequents. The symbol '$\Rightarrow$' may be read as 'implies', so the rules could also be read as 'A implies X', although in a strict logical sense this may not be true.

Table 4.1 Some sample rules to illustrate forward and backward chaining

Rule number	Rule	
1	A	$\Rightarrow X$
2	B	$\Rightarrow Y$
3	C & D	$\Rightarrow Z$
4	E & B	$\Rightarrow W$
5	Z	$\Rightarrow H$
6	X	$\Rightarrow B$
7	F & W	$\Rightarrow Z$

There are two types of inference that are commonly applied to expert systems, forward and backward chaining. Forward chaining runs from the antecedent to the consequent, in the direction of the arrow.

Example 1 In this example, suppose we had data 'B, C, E'. This would be stored in the working memory, which we shall denote by a box, thus:

> B, C, E

Looking down the list of rules in Table 4.1, we see that rule 2 is satisfied since its antecedent B is in the working memory. So, that rule may be 'fired', by which we mean that its consequent, Y, is now assumed to be true and can be added to the working memory:

```
B, C, E
Y
```

Continuing the inspection of the rules, we see that rule 4 can also be fired, adding W to the list of known facts.

```
B, C, E
Y
W
```

Proceeding further down the list shows that no more rules can be fired. Starting at the top and looking down the list once more does not add any more information to the list of known facts.

Example 2   Let us take another example. Suppose the original set of data is 'C, D, E, X'.

```
C, D, E, X
```

Scanning down the list shows that rule 3 may be triggered straight away, so that Z is now one of the known facts. (In this context, 'triggering' means that the antecedent of the rule has been matched and that it can now be fired, ie its consequent added to the collection of known facts.)

```
C, D, E, X
Z
```

With this additional information, we can also trigger rule 5 to conclude H.

```
C, D, E, X
Z
H
```

This rule could not have been fired under the original set of data. Further inspection shows that rule 6 may also be fired, adding B to the list of known facts.

```
C, D, E, X
Z
H
B
```

With this extra information in hand, we may check down the full set of rules once more and observe that rules 2 and 4 may now be fired on this, the second pass.

```
C, D, E, X
Z
H
B
Y
W
```

Further passes through the rules would add nothing new.

At the start of this chapter, we mentioned the three components of an expert system and now we are in a better position to understand their role. The rule base is equivalent to the collection of rules in Table 4.1 and the working memory is used and updated like the small boxes in the text. The control strategy is a little more complex.

Consider again these two examples. In the first, one pass through the rules provided all the inferences that could be made. But in the second example, a second pass through the rules furnished further inferences and added more facts to the working memory. Had there only been one pass through the rules on the second example, the outcome of the inference procedure would have been different. The order in which the rules are executed and the number of passes through the rules are part of the control strategy. Suppose a control strategy had been: *Make only one pass through the rules*. The state of working memory at the end of the consultation (ie after a single pass) would be the same as above. But for the second example, the final state would have been different, ie

```
C, D, E, X
Z
H
B
```

and not

```
C, D, E, X
Z
H
B
Y
W
```

Other variations on the control strategy are possible, eg *Make a single pass through the rules and fire no more than one rule*.

Control strategies like this are appropriate in some circumstances, usually where the rules have been ordered carefully in advance. For example, so that the most general rules come at the top of the list.

The order in which the rules are stored in the rule base can have an effect on the efficiency of the expert system. Suppose we re-order the rules in Table 4.1 so that rules whose antecedents do not appear in the consequent of other rules come at the head of the list, and rules whose consequents do not appear in the antecedents of other rules come at the end of the list.

The data from example 2, 'C, D, E, X' will now fire all the required rules on a single pass, as the reader may verify.

It is important to warn here that it might not always be possible to re-order the rules so as to improve the performance of the expert system in the way that Table 4.2 might suggest. As the number of rules increases together with the complexity of their interconnections and the number of clauses in the rules, so it becomes more difficult to partition cleanly the antecedent-only and consequent-only data items. Heuristic strategies may be adopted to improve the ordering of the rules, but it is a problem of rule-based systems that the order of the rules can affect not only the efficiency of execution of the expert system, but also the conclusions which it might reach. The control strategy needs to consider the ordering of the rules as well as the number of passes.

Table 4.2 Table 4.1 re-ordered

Old rule number	New rule number	Rule	
1	1	A	$\Rightarrow$ X
3	2	C & D	$\Rightarrow$ Z
6	3	X	$\Rightarrow$ B
4	4	E & B	$\Rightarrow$ W
7	5	F & W	$\Rightarrow$ Z
2	6	B	$\Rightarrow$ Y
5	7	Z	$\Rightarrow$ H

4.4 Backward chaining

Forward chaining works by matching the known data against the antecedents of the rules and observing what further conclusions may be drawn. Backward chaining, by contrast, matches known or hypothesised conclusions against the consequents of the rules, to determine what states of the world could have given rise to them.

As an example, let us suppose that B is a hypothesis. This must be matched against the *consequent* of one of the rules. In order to show that B is true, it would be enough to show that rule 6 had fired, and for rule 6 to fire, X should have been true. Matching against the consequent of rule 1 shows that for X to be true, A should be true. Hence, we may infer that to show that B is true, we need to show that X is true, and to show that X is true, show that A is true.

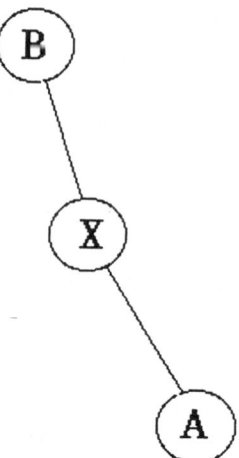

Figure 4.2 The backward chaining tree to prove B

The proposition that is to be proved is at the root of the tree, by convention drawn at the top of the page. The terminal nodes (leaves) are drawn at the bottom of the page. They represent the facts that should be gathered from the world.

The easiest way to illustrate such chains of reasoning is by a tree (*see* Figure 4.2). Note that the goal that is ultimately to be proved is written at the top of the page, ie the root of the tree.

A more complex example concerns proving the truth of H. We can see straight away from Table 4.1 that H is true if Z is true from rule 5. The next step would be to prove Z, but there are two possible ways to do this, either by matching against the consequent of rule 3 or rule 7. So, Z may be proved in either of two ways, but the steps involved in proving Z increase dramatically, and a tree becomes essential to keep track of them all (*see* Figure 4.3).

Handling backward chaining efficiently is a much more complex task than executing forward chaining. Again, we shall use an example to illustrate some of the difficulties. Refer to Figure 4.3 and Table 4.1.

Suppose we have in Working Memory the data F, E, C, D and wish to prove H.

F, E, C, D
Prove H

Figure 4.3 generates the hypothesis Z, which may be proved by showing that F and W are both true.

F, E, C, D
Prove H
Hyp Z
Hyp F
Hyp W

Fortunately F is part of the original data, so that may be marked as true and attention turned to proving W, which is not in the starting data.

```
F, E, C, D
Prove H
Hyp Z
Hyp F true
Hyp W
```

Figure 4.3 shows that W may be proved by showing E and B are true.

```
F, E, C, D
Prove H
Hyp Z
Hyp F true
Hyp W
Hyp E
Hyp B
```

Checking the original data again shows that E is true, but we need to look further to find out about B, ie show that X is true.

```
F, E, C, D
Prove H
Hyp Z
Hyp F true
Hyp W
Hyp E true
Hyp B
Hyp X
```

X is not part of the original data, so we need to see how to prove X, ie by proving A.

```
F, E, C, D
Prove H
Hyp Z
Hyp F true
Hyp W
Hyp E true
Hyp B
Hyp X
Hyp A
```

Sadly, A is not part of the data, nor is there any other way of proving A to be true. So, we have to abandon that method of proving X, and of proving B and so on. The hypothesis tree has to

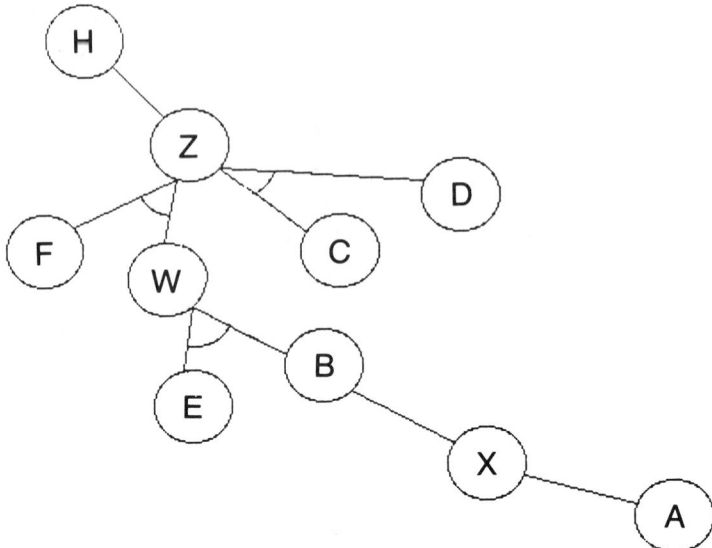

Figure 4.3 The backward chaining tree to prove H

be traced back until we find a point at which to resume our search for the proof of H. This process is known as backtracking. When the backtrack is complete, the working memory will look like:

```
F, E, C, D
Prove H
Hyp Z
```

Looking at the other options for proving Z, we have:

```
F, E, C, D
Prove H
Hyp Z
Hyp C
Hyp D
```

These last two hypotheses are included in the original data, so we may mark Z as true, and hence H as true.

```
F, E, C, D
Prove H true
Hyp Z true
Hyp C true
Hyp D true
```

This exposition of backward chaining has glossed over many of the difficult technical problems of handling backtracking efficiently. Indeed, research is continuing to improve backtracking algorithms. For instance, in the example above, much effort could have been saved if the shorter proof for C & D had been checked first, before heading off to try fruitlessly to prove W. The format of Working Memory displayed in the example gave no clue to the relationship between the various hypotheses, whether one was a sub-hypothesis to another, or whether they were *And* or *Or* clauses. So, the information from Figure 4.3 or Table 4.1 would still be required.

It would not be a good idea, therefore, for someone who is starting out in expert systems to begin by trying to write their own backwards chaining expert system. Commercially written shells are available to offer that facility and when trying to produce a useful, demonstrable expert system in a short time, it is always wise to adopt a low-risk approach. The examples above are intended to demonstrate how these techniques work and are not to be taken as recipes for how to construct something similar.

4.5 Simplified inference methods for process control

In the context of control, If . . . Then rules are used to indicate which control actions should be carried out in particular circumstances. The antecedent of the rule defines the situation, ie the state of the world, and the consequent defines the recommended control action. For control the rule is If ⟨*situation*⟩ Then ⟨*action*⟩.

Immediately, we can see that only forward chaining will be needed for simple control. For a particular state of the world, the rule indicates what action should be taken. Backward chaining would be needed were the question posed as 'Under what states of the world would this control action be taken?'. We shall discuss circumstances under which questions of this type would arise, but not for everyday control. Hence, an important simplification has been made, which should ease the programming task considerably.

The next simplification is to do with the length of the chains of inference. In the forward chaining examples above, the same fact could appear as a part of the antecedents or the consequents, such as B, X and W in Table 4.1. This means that the rules may give rise to chains of inference, where the consequent of one or more rules forms the antecedent to others. Within control, there is the distinction between observed and controlled variables. When the observed and controlled variables form two disjoint sets, then the antecedent will be defined strictly from the variables of one set and the consequent from the other. Therefore, there is no possibility of the rules forming chains.

Hence, we may conclude that for simple control, a single, forward inference is enough. This makes the programming task very straightforward, since most of the extra features provided by general purpose commercial expert system shells are not needed. Also, this simplification means that the programs may be written to run very efficiently and compactly. The small size of the programs means that the rule-base need not be stored externally, but can be incorporated within the program. This might seem to compromise the earlier definition of an expert system, but the separate nature of the rules is maintained.

Backward chaining has its uses too, in domains where hypothesis generation predominates, such as in fault diagnosis. For this kind of application, the expert system could adopt the approach of supposing a particular fault exists and looking for evidence to support that hypothesis, via backward chaining.

Again, for some applications it is better to take a mixed strategy using both forward and backward chaining. Suppose an expert system is operating in an environment where little data is available at the start of the consultation, but more could be acquired by querying the user. The expert system has to be designed so that it does not query the user more than necessary and, especially, does not ask for the same information more than once. To do that would irritate the user and cause a loss of confidence in the expert system's conclusions. Under these circumstances, the expert system could start off by reasoning forwards from the data it has available to see if any conclusions may be reached. These could even be reported to the user. If no final conclusions are available, the expert system could choose a hypothesis to try to prove and use backward reasoning to generate sub-hypotheses. The sub-hypotheses could be checked by querying the user directly. If one of these hypotheses turns out not to be true, the expert system could revert to forward reasoning to see if any other inferences could be drawn from the data recently acquired. This could lead directly to a suitable conclusion, or could indicate another hypothesis suitable for investigation under backward chaining.

Table 4.3 Some rules to illustrate a mixed forward and backward chaining strategy

Rule number	Rule	
1	G	$\Rightarrow$ K
2	G & M	$\Rightarrow$ J
3	M	$\Rightarrow$ V
4	Q & N	$\Rightarrow$ R
5	S & T	$\Rightarrow$ R
6	T & P	$\Rightarrow$ U
7	L & K	$\Rightarrow$ N
8	J	$\Rightarrow$ P

Let us consider another short example, drawn from Table 4.3. *See* also Figure 4.4. Suppose the starting condition for the Working Memory is G, L, T. Under forward chaining, the first pass through the rules adds K to Working Memory, which may be used to infer

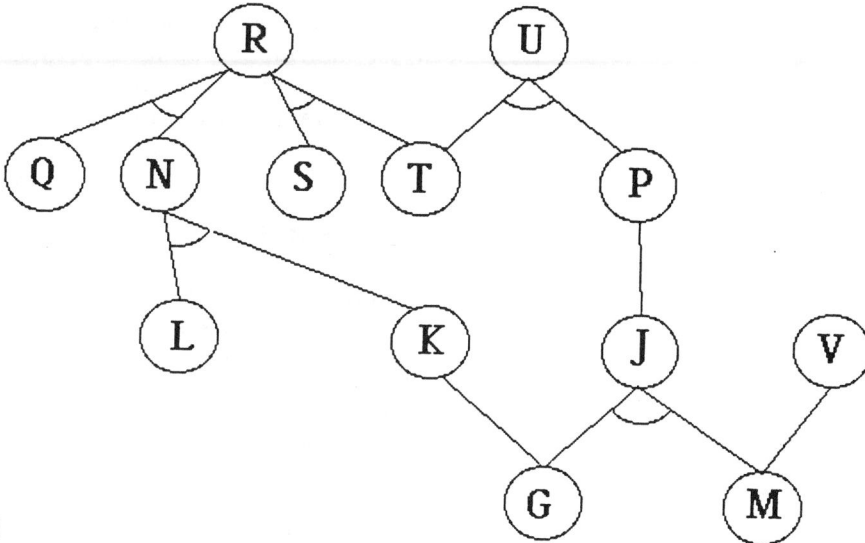

Figure 4.4 Table 4.3 re-expressed

N. That is as far as forward chaining can go for now. So, let us look at what backward chaining might accomplish.

> G, L, T
> K, N

Before any backward chaining can be done, the expert system would have to choose which goal to prove. Figure 4.4 shows that there are three goals, ie R, U, and V. If these had been pre-assigned a priority rating, then it would be simple enough to pick one and try to prove it, but in the absence of such a priority some other decision strategy would have to be used. Four rules each have one clause proven true, ie 2, 4, 5 and 6, so it might be worth trying to prove the other clause of these, viz M, Q, S, P. At this point, we could randomly pick one of the four to prove, or look again at Figure 4.4 to make the selection as useful as possible. Q and S both appear in only one rule each, so we could say that proving either of them will only enable us to draw one inference. P is in the antecedent of only one rule, but M is in the antecedent of two rules, one of which leads to a final conclusion. Since there is no priority on the final conclusions, it would be most advantageous to try to prove M. So, Working Memory might look like:

> G, L, T
> K, N
> Prove M

Since M is not the consequent of another rule, the only way to acquire information about it is to ask the expert system user directly. Suppose this is done, and an affirmative answer obtained. Working Memory would look like:

```
G, L, T
K, N
Prove M true
```

Forward chaining may now resume and quite a cascade of inferences are enabled:

```
G, L, T
K, N
Prove M true
J
V
P
U
```

These extra inferences have been obtained fortuitously, because only two inferences had been anticipated after the rather cursory inspection of the inference network as described in the previous paragraph. At this point, two of the final conclusions have been proved, so they could be reported to the user, perhaps with a request on whether the consultation should continue.

Continuing the consultation would return to backward chaining. There are only two rules now that remain partly proven, 4 and 5, both of which have R as their consequent. To complete the consultation, the user could be asked whether either or both of Q and S are true.

For any expert system, whether mixed initiative or not, the decision whether to adopt forward or backward chaining has to do with whether data or hypotheses predominate. If data are plentiful, then it is best to let the expert system carry out forward chaining, reporting significant conclusions to the user. Where data may be obtained at some cost, it is better to concentrate on using the hypotheses efficiently and letting them drive the consultation. Some ranking of the hypotheses could be very useful to make sure that the most important hypotheses were checked first, according to whatever local criterion is selected.

4.6 Extending the expert system architecture

So far, this chapter has concentrated on how the expert system might acquire data from the outside world and combine the data with the contents of its knowledge base to reach conclusions about the state of the world. However, it is unlikely that the users will remain satisfied for long with such a restricted use of the expert

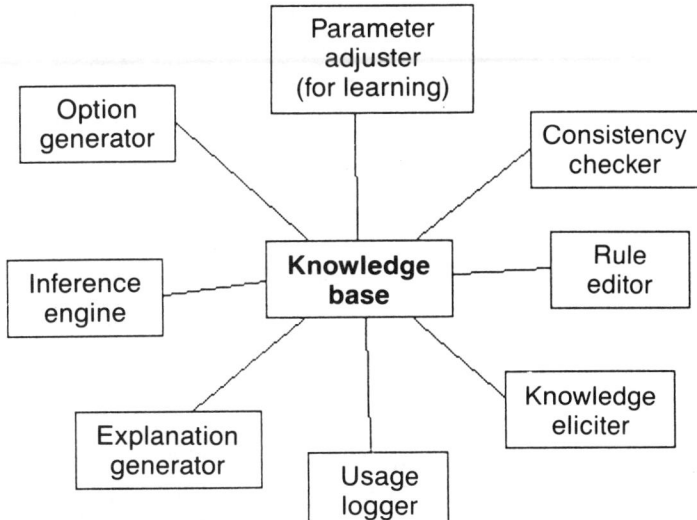

Figure 4.5 Other possible facilities in an expert system

system. After all, the knowledge it contains is an important resource within the organisation and it is worthwhile providing other facilities to enable that knowledge to be used in an effective way.

This section will look at some of the possibilities (*see* Figure 4.5). No doubt the reader will think of yet more.

Amending the rule base

During the processes of constructing and maintaining the expert system, the user will need to check the rules, to try to identify conflict and repetition amongst the rules. A good rule-editor would contain facilities like:

– Produce ordered lists of antecedent and consequent clauses, with a list of clauses that appear in both. This would help identify clauses that were similar in appearance, whether deliberately or not. The user would need to check whether similarity of meaning had been intended. Clauses that appear in both lists enable chains of reasoning.
– Carry out a heuristic re-ordering of the rules. This might be along the lines of that demonstrated at Table 4.2, where efficiency of execution was the requirement, but other re-ordering strategies might be required, such as grouping together rules that concern the same part of the domain because, for example, they all contain the same clause, whether as antecedent or consequent. Re-grouping in this way might not be strictly possible, in the sense of

partitioning the rule-base cleanly, but a heuristic approximation would be helpful.

– Syntax guiding. The syntax of rules is well defined and a rule editor could guide the user to construct only well-formed rules, by providing a short menu of options each time a clause has been entered. The contents of the menu would depend on how far the user had progressed through the rule, but syntax guidance would mean avoiding a tiresome compilation cycle. This is analogous to the difference between using a compiled or an interpreted programming language.

Accessing other programs

While an expert system is running, it would be irritating if it had to query the user for a piece of information which had to be obtained by running another program, such as a database, spreadsheet or model. Much better then if the expert system has access to other frequently used programs as well. This could be done in the background, so that the user is not aware of the expert system's interaction. The user would only be aware of interacting with the expert system, since it is controlling its access elsewhere.

However, access need not be confined to other programs which are run transparently. Some expert systems have been constructed that access videotex, video disks and speech generators as the best way to explain to the user what the expert system's conclusions are. For example, Delta used video disk to explain procedures in diesel locomotive maintenance. LINKman relies heavily on displays of graphs of trends in process variables. All these enhance the display of information to the user.

Explanation

Some definitions of expert systems place great emphasis on the ability of the expert system to explain its line reasoning to the user. This should ensure that the user has confidence in the expert system's conclusion and would be willing, therefore, to act on its recommendation. Also, if the expert system's reasoning is faulty, because of insufficient or erroneous knowledge and/or data, then the user has the right to reject the expert system's advice. One of the main reasons for choosing a rule-based knowledge representation format is the belief that rules are easily expressed and understood by domain experts.

The earliest commercial expert system shells generated explanations by tracing the line of reasoning that the expert system had followed. This often meant tracing all the blind alleys that the backward chainer had followed, which made bewildering reading for the user and did not have the required effect of increasing confidence.

Text-based explanations are easily generated, but they are not the best way to convey complex information. As we have already seen with Table 4.3 and Figure 4.4, the information contained in rules can be re-expressed much more intelligibly as a graph. Hence, we could expect that animated graphs would interest, explain and entertain much more effectively.

It should not be overlooked that another of the overall goals in constructing an expert system is to help in the training of the work force. Good explanations are essential for this task. Also, it is worth introducing various optional levels of detail into the explanation. So, when a panic is on, the user can obtain a quick, succinct explanation of why the expert system suggests a particular course of action. When the crisis has passed, the user might want to go back over the situation and query the expert system more closely as to why it reached that conclusion.

However, the level of explanation that a rule-based expert system could generate is constrained by the knowledge represented in the rules. A rule-based expert system has no knowledge of the world and its manipulation of the rules is purely syntactical. If better explanation of actions are required, the expert system builder would need to write them in, attached to special-purpose explanation procedures. Any method that relies on the designer thinking of every possible question is bound to be incomplete and would require a great deal of effort to construct.

By their nature rules are shallow and superficial. The explanations they generate will be like that too.

4.7 Other inference methods and architectures

For the sake of completeness, we shall cover briefly some of the other techniques that have been suggested.

Heuristic search

Earlier, the distinction was made between classificatory and synthetic expert systems. Classificatory systems use inference techniques such as forward and backward chaining, while synthetic systems have to search through a large search space of possible solutions.

For complex domains, the amount of search that might be needed is enormous, well beyond what could be achieved within a useful time interval. Many ways exist to cut down the amount of search that must be done in order to find a satisfactory solution. One of these is heuristic search.

As already mentioned, heuristic knowledge is domain-specific knowledge, derived from experience. In classificatory expert systems, it would be represented in the rule-base and used to infer conclusions. In synthetic expert systems, heuristic knowledge may be used in a different way, ie to guide the direction of the search.

Search problems boil down to finding the quickest path to the best solution, but if that can't be done, then finding a quick enough path to a good enough solution. This means that blind alleys should be avoided, and if a slight detour from the apparently direct route would give a better answer then the detour should be followed. Straightforward arithmetic methods can be used to guide the search path, but they cannot cope well with recommending useful detours. Some background knowledge of the domain is needed and that is where the heuristics come in. They can be used to augment or replace arithmetic methods for guiding search.

Non-monotonic reasoning

In many everyday situations, we are obliged to reason with incomplete or dubious information. We use a mixture of common sense and other scraps of knowledge to piece together a picture of the world which is adequate for making some decisions. We make guesses about what the state of the world is, perhaps do a few experiments and then integrate the new knowledge with what we already know or believe, revising assumptions and beliefs in a more or less reasonable manner.

Formal systems, on the other hand, lack breadth of knowledge and do not yet have satisfactory mechanisms for reasoning under uncertainty. The familiar logical systems reason from a basic set of premises to reach conclusions, with each newly inferred fact added to the store of beliefs. The number of known facts will always increase monotonically, ie no facts will be removed from the collection. This is true of the inference systems described in this book.

However, monotonic reasoning is not necessarily the only way to reason. As explained above, people often make assumptions, draw conclusions, perform tests, subsequently to withdraw the intermediate conclusions and their underlying assumptions. Hence, the number of believed facts can decrease as well as increase, ie vary non-monotonically.

Non-monotonic reasoning seeks to provide formal structures within which the inference system can make assumptions, acquire new data from the world, identify conflicts between the new data and existing beliefs and identify which assumptions need to be retracted, together with their dependent conclusions. Truth maintenance systems (TMS), or belief revision systems, have been built and are becoming much more efficient.

Non-monotonic reasoning and TMSs are likely to be useful in the future, because they can cope with unreliable data. In process control, faulty sensors can mislead the fault diagnoser, so the ability of TMSs to trace how beliefs were formed and resolve subsequent conflicts could be important. It should be emphasised that TMSs are not simple and in particular every belief must record its justifications, ie those beliefs on which it is founded. Furthermore, the statements that are not currently believed must also be retained should their status change in the future.

Inference with structured objects

Structured objects group together different kinds of knowledge, so that inference procedures can easily access whatever is required for a particular problem-solving task. It should be mentioned that structured objects are usually designed specifically for certain kinds of tasks, but are often extensible should a slightly different but related problem occur.

Apart from associating knowledge together, frames also have internal structure which can be used during inference. Frames might appear similar to records in a database, but the slots of a frame can be made active, ie a procedure is automatically invoked if the contents of the slot are changed. For example, an *if-added* procedure indicated what should be done if a slot is filled. Other procedures attached to slots can indicate what should be done to determine how the slot should be filled. When a new frame is created, its attached procedures can supply the values of some of the slots, for example, by inheritance from parent frames, querying the user or other programs or devices, or by supplying a default value.

There are many ways in which frames can be applied to different problems. The power of a particular application lies in the ways in which knowledge has been represented and is utilised by the program. As we have seen, the knowledge may be represented as facts within the frame structure, but also as associated procedures that are invoked appropriately. The goal of the AI researcher is to provide facilities for representing knowledge that are applicable in many domains, so that new applications can be set up with the minimum of re-representation. The basic AI inference techniques can be re-used, but the knowledge should be represented in such a way that it too may be applied to new applications.

Blackboard architectures

Blackboard expert systems adopt a different style to that depicted in Figure 4.1 (*see* Figure 4.6). The expert system consists of separate 'knowledge sources' (like experts), which contain the domain knowledge, and a blackboard to which all the knowledge

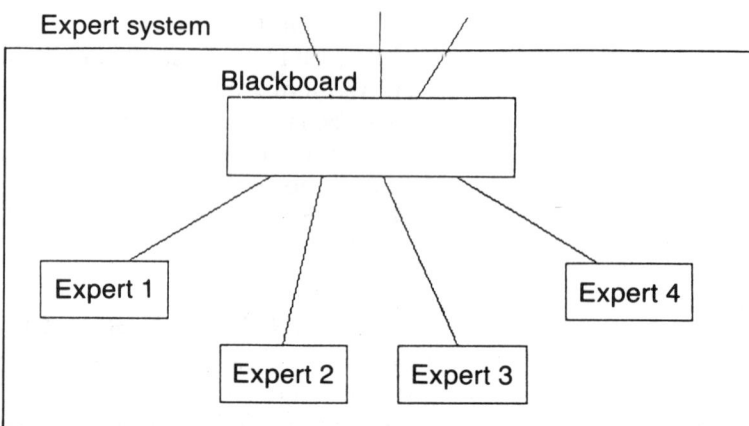

*Figure 4.6 A blackboard
architecture*

sources have access. As data or a fact appears on the blackboard, the knowledge sources check to see if they can use that fact to fire some of their rules. If so, a knowledge source may add data to the blackboard, add or modify hypotheses, update the facts or whatever its speciaility. Once a knowledge source is activated, it operates on the blackboard without interruption until it is finished. The knowledge sources only communicate with each other via the blackboard.

Each knowledge source monitors the blackboard awaiting something on which it can act. This style of behaviour is similar to that of a *demon*, which is like a procedure that watches for some condition to become true and then activates a process.

Blackboard architectures are popular in applications that run continuously and receive data from many sources. Examples are in process monitoring and in battlefield conditions. This kind of problem is known as 'data fusion' or 'sensor fusion'. As data enter the system, hypotheses may be presented on the blackboard, which other knowledge sources can use to postulate evidence, the presence or absence of which can serve to modify the likelihood of a hypothesis. Such problems are also real-time.

Multiple expert systems and distributed AI

Another possible architecture is that of multiple expert systems (*see* Figure 4.7). In the blackboard architecture, only one knowledge source operates at a time, but with multiple expert systems, more than one expert system may be at work at any time. Communication between expert systems need not be limited to be via the single channel of the blackboard. Such systems are extremely complex to verify or validate. Conflict resolution

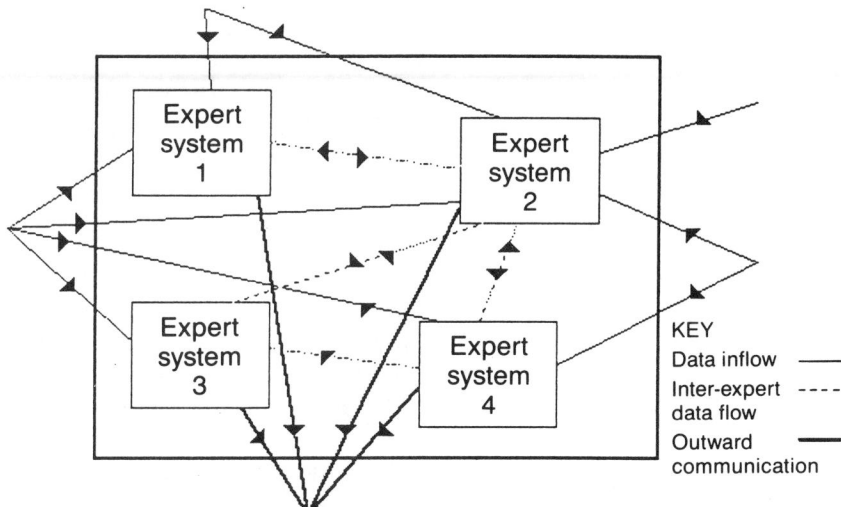

Figure 4.7 Multiple expert systems

between the interacting expert systems is a problem of its own – what to do if two expert systems come up with contradictory conclusions?

Multiple-motive expert systems

This is another refinement to expert systems, likely to be addressed in the future when many of today's problems have been solved. A multiple-motive expert system would be capable of dealing with a steady flow of sensor data and be able to react to them in real-time. However, instead of addressing itself to a single problem, it would have several problems to solve and would have to select which to solve at any time. The multiple motives would not necessarily be consistent and new information and interruptions might require radical re-ordering of plans and goals. The surrounding world might be hazardous, events moving quickly and decisions made urgently. Such an expert system is difficult to imagine now, because we are still so vague about what it should do, never mind how it might do it. However, it is more likely to resemble a small child or an animal than anything else in human experience so far.

4.8 Rules right or wrong

This chapter and the previous one have discussed rules in some detail, covering some of the ways they can be used to construct expert systems. In order to give a balanced picture, we should also look at some of their weaknesses, so that the reader can be warned against repeating some avoidable mistakes.

As a knowledge representation format, If . . . Then rules have very little inherent structure. There are no in built constraints on what should go in the antecedent and what in the consequent. This has led to a 'bucket' approach to programming, under the naive belief that so long as it is expressed as a rule somehow, and both forward and backward reasoning are available, then the knowledge will get used and everything will be all right. All the knowledge is brought together, thrown into the bucket and given a good stir. No experienced programmer would adopt such an approach to constructing and maintaining a Pascal or Fortran program, and so there is no justification for treating rule-based programs in that way either.

Since rules lack structure, then some structure must be imposed, in the same way that structured programming imposes a structure on a conventional program. There are several ways of choosing a structure, for example, grouping rules according to the part of the domain to which they refer, or ordering them according to their generality. The Chocolate Biscuit and Blue Circle case studies both structure the rules, but in different ways.

A structure needs to be imposed on the rules for two main reasons. Firstly, the way in which the rules are presented in the rule-base could affect the conclusions which a consultation with the expert system reaches and second, the rule-base needs to be maintained by humans, so their access to the rules has to be rendered effective. We have already mentioned how tools could help here.

One of the alleged joys of rule-based programming was its incremental nature, ie when another piece of knowledge is acquired, it is added to the rule-base by just typing it in, with no need to edit a large program, re-compile, de-bug etc. This is true, but software engineering has been striving for some time towards independence of software modules precisely in order to limit the need for unnecessary effort in maintaining and debugging programs. But the emphasis on incrementality also encourages the belief in bucket programming, with the hope that more and more morsels of knowledge can be dropped into the bucket to swirl happily around. Instead, as new knowledge is acquired, the expert system maintainer needs to examine the contents of the rule-base to check that the rule is consistent with the other rules already there. So, incrementing the rule-base needs to be done carefully, with the help of editing tools.

Good editing tools can support the programmer while editing the rule base, but the programmer needs to establish whether the rule is meaningful and appropriate for the purpose. An editor can help, by carrying out character by character matches with other clauses, but a rule-based expert system cannot by itself check whether the rule is valid or not. Its treatment of the rules is purely syntactic, just as a string of characters, with no meaning attached.

It is the job of the humans who use and interact with the expert system to supply the semantic information.

The shallowness of the expert system's knowledge has other important effects. As already discussed, it is limited in the kinds of explanations that may be produced. If some novel situation were to occur that was not covered by the expert system's rules, then there is a problem. The expert system might not realise that it has met a new situation and would give inappropriate advice. The standard example uses the rules and fact:

> If x is a bird, then x can fly.
> If x is a penguin, then x is a bird.
> Joe is a penguin.

to conclude

> Joe is a bird, Joe can fly.

Our experience tells us that penguins cannot fly, and that the rule about birds and flying does not accurately cover all cases. The first reaction might be to extend the rule by adding another clause:

> If x is a bird & x is not a penguin, then x can fly.

This is a dangerous path to follow, because soon the rule becomes cluttered with lots of inelegant clauses to cover all the other exceptions we might think of, such as kiwis and emus and whether the bird has a broken wing and is awake and has learnt how to fly . . . As explained in the previous chapter, frames provide facilities to handle exceptions.

The bird example above indicates another problem with rules, namely that they are just not suitable for representing some kinds of knowledge. An expert doctor or engineer does not remember his lifetime's experience as a collection of If . . . Then rules. Experts have conceptual models of human anatomy or how an engine works which could not be represented feasibly using rules. One need only look at the enormous number of ways humans use to convey information to one another to get an idea of the limitations of rules, such as maps, musical notation, circuit diagrams, graphs, three-dimensional models, pictures, recipes etc.

The rules that prevail in process control are subject to other difficulties that need to be seriously considered. Many of the rules are based on empirical observation and express known correlations between situations and outcomes. Let us look again at two of the rules from Table 4.3.

> 4 Q & N $\Rightarrow$ R
> 5 S & T $\Rightarrow$ R

During the example, we wanted to prove R. If these rules had been strict logical implications, it would have been necessary only to show either that Q & N was true *or* that S & T was true. There would have been no need to have checked both rules. If Q & N was true, then R would be true and that would be that. Furthermore, knowing R to be true tells us nothing at all about the truth of S & T. All this follows from the logic of implication.

Such a situation would not normally hold in the real world. Few implications can be that certain. Normally, if there were two ways to prove a goal, we would check both, just in case there were some other unconsidered clause to the rule that had thwarted the truth of the goal. The representation and manipulation of these and other uncertainties is keeping researchers happily occupied.

Rules have their problems, but they have some definite advantages too. Parts of the knowledge of a domain can be readily expressed as rules. And this seems to be true particularly for the case of process control. This could be due to the fact that quite a lot of process control relies upon the skills of human operators, who have practised their skills so often. When operators describe to one another how they perform their tasks, rules are the natural medium for expression. The operators may or may not possess deep knowledge about the process they are controlling, but rules are a compact, 'compiled' way to present it, even if the operators do not consciously use rules as they go about their day's work.

Rule-based programming is fairly straightforward, so it would be possible to write a tailored expert system without too much trouble. This would not be advisable since many rule-based shells are available on the market, which can be used to put an expert system together very quickly. This is a much better way to try out the technology, construct a prototype and design and build from there.

The simple programming means that a rule-based program can execute very quickly. The separate rule-base allows the rules to be changed quickly and easily, so that prototype versions can be constructed and tested, on-line if necessary.

Rule-based expert systems are suitable in domains where the knowledge is fairly accessible and shallow. It also helps if there is not too much of it, because a very large rule-base would be difficult to construct and maintain. They are also well suited to process control because they can be written to execute quickly, which is important in real-time applications. In such situations, the number of rules is not likely to be very great anyway. When trying to decide if a rule-based expert system is the tool for the task, it is sensible to find out if rules are available. If they are not, it is either because the domain knowledge is too complex or vague to be expressed as rules or nobody knows how to control the process. In the latter case, trying to get an expert system to do it is not going to help.

Chapter 5 The Chocolate Biscuit Factory

5.1 Introduction

The Chocolate Biscuit Factory is an imaginary example designed to illustrate some of the uses of expert systems. The reader is asked to imagine a chocolate biscuit factory which suffers some elderly and unsatisfactory plant. By contrast, the latest thing in expert system technology is about to be installed.

5.2 Knowledge representation

The expert system which the factory has chosen to install has a rule-based knowledge representation format. It has been tailored in some ways to suit domains which require the diagnosis and repair of faults. The factory is troubled by faults and breakdowns but the operators and tradesmen are quite good at diagnosing what has gone wrong. Frequently, they observe a defect on the production line, which could suggest several possible causes. These can be checked out until one or more breakdowns have been identified.

The rule-based format of knowledge representation has other benefits because it makes explanations easier and more intelligible. This is intended to lead to a better trained and more capable workforce.

Occasionally, an operator on one of the machines in the chocolate biscuit factory notices something going wrong with the chocolate or the biscuits. These observations are called *triggers* because they trigger a suspicion in the operator's mind that a fault is developing. A class of rule is constructed which has the following format.

IF ⟨*trigger*⟩ THEN SUGGEST ⟨*hypothesis*⟩

Hypotheses here are things like 'oven too hot', which link a fault in a piece of equipment to an observed effect, such as runny chocolate. Some triggers suggest a single hypothesis, but others could suggest more than one. So, the operator observes a trigger, which could indicate one or more possible hypotheses.

The hypotheses have to be caused by something in the plant, so another class of rule is needed:

⟨*hypothesis*⟩ CAUSED BY ⟨*fault*⟩

For example,

oven too hot CAUSED BY gas temperature too high

The hypothesis is the mechanism which links a fault on the

plant to the trigger. If someone asked 'Why does high gas temperature make the chocolate runny?', the answer lies in the hypothesis – 'Because the oven is too hot'.

The operator needs a way of checking whether the fault has occurred or not, so a test has to be applied. The proper test is given by a rule of the format:

⟨fault⟩ CONFIRMED BY *⟨test⟩*

If the test fails, then that fault is ruled out. But if the test succeeds, then some action must be taken. The action might be a simple repair or in the case of something more complex, calling a skilled repairman or reporting the fault to a shift supervisor before discarding a batch of product. Thus, another type of rule is needed to provide the appropriate action:

IF *⟨fault⟩* THEN DO *⟨action⟩*

The knowledge representation format outlined above uses five different kinds of object in the knowledge base. The *trigger* is the observation that first causes the operator to notice that something is going wrong. This could suggest several *hypotheses* to the skilled fitter or repairman. Each hypothesis could be caused by one or more *faults*. Each fault can be checked by a *test* and if the fault is confirmed, then some *action* needs to be taken.

These five objects are linked together by four kinds of rule (*see* Table 5.1). *See* section 5.12 for lists of the five classes of object.

Table 5.1 Rule formats

IF	*⟨trigger⟩*	THEN SUGGEST	*⟨hypothesis⟩*	ITS
	⟨hypothesis⟩	CAUSED BY	*⟨fault⟩*	CAU
	⟨fault⟩	CONFIRMED BY	*⟨test⟩*	CON
IF	*⟨fault⟩*	THEN DO	*⟨action⟩*	ITD

Four kinds of rules are needed to represent the different kinds of knowledge that exist. The first rule uses data to suggest a hypothesis, but the second uses a hypothesis to suggest data. The third kind of rule provides basic information of how to test for a particular kind of fault, but the fourth says that in those circumstances where a fault is confirmed then a particular action should be done (*see* Figure 5.1).

5.3 Knowledge elicitation

The knowledge engineer feels happy that the knowledge representation format and inference mechanisms are suitable for the chocolate biscuit factory and so embarks on a process of knowledge elicitation. This is not a straightforward task, because

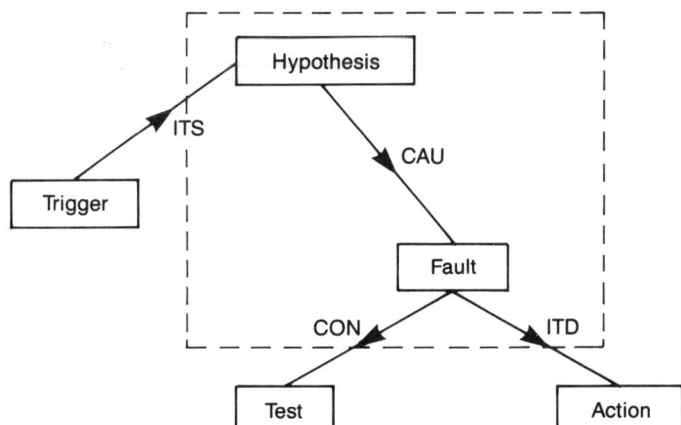

Figure 5.1 Structure of the rule-base

The dashed line indicates the separation between the external world and the expert system.

so many different people have pieces of relevant knowledge. The operators can describe most of the triggers, but sometimes leave it to the fitters to find out what has really gone wrong. The first list of triggers is usually incomplete, but after talking to some of the other people involved, other items can be added. Knowledge elicitation and acquisition could carry on for ever, because new knowledge can always be learned, but at some point enough knowledge will be gathered for the expert system to be prototyped, perhaps with better versions to follow later.

The next job is to compile a list of faults. If a log of faults is kept, then this simplifies the task, but otherwise it is a matter of interviewing the repairman and fitters to find out what jobs they do.

Given these two lists, the rules can be elicited by asking for the links between the two. This can turn out to be an exercise in knowledge refining, because the experts find that having to sit down and think and explain what they do helps them to find new links or think more carefully about the old ones.

The next stages are fairly straightforward. Each fault may be tested in some way or another. Sometimes, the test may be quite simple, but other times it might involve laboratory tests or queries to suppliers. Whatever the case, some action must be taken. The shift managers can be helpful here. They might have been trying to impose some discipline and consistency on the operators' response to faults and this gives them a chance to review their recommendations and put them down as rules.

The above account of a knowledge elicitation task makes it sound very simple and easy. In reality, all sorts of things can go wrong. Operators might be resentful of a computer program daring to take over the skills which they are proud to protect. Knowledge

Table 5.2 The trigger-hypothesis rules: IF ⟨*trigger*⟩ THEN SUGGEST ⟨*hypothesis*⟩

Rule number	Trigger	Hypothesis
ITS1	biscuits pale	oven too cool
ITS2	biscuits not risen	oven too cool
ITS3	biscuits burnt	oven too hot
ITS4	biscuits burnt	too much cocoa
ITS5	biscuits burnt	too much sugar
ITS6	biscuits not risen	too much cocoa
ITS7	biscuits not risen	too little raising agent
ITS8	biscuits not risen	faulty flour
ITS9	biscuits pale	wrong sugar
ITS10	biscuits pale	faulty flour
ITS11	chocolate sticky	not enough air in mixture
ITS12	chocolate sticky	faulty cocoa
ITS13	chocolate bubbling	oven too hot
ITS14	chocolate runny	rancid butter
ITS15	chocolate runny	factory too warm
ITS16	chocolate too dark	too much cocoa
ITS17	chocolate too light	wrong sugar
ITS18	bad smell	rancid butter
ITS19	bad smell	*check* biscuits burnt

Table 5.3 The hypothesis-fault rules: ⟨*hypothesis*⟩ CAUSED BY ⟨*fault*⟩

Rule number	Hypothesis	Fault
CAU1	faulty flour	change of source
CAU2	faulty flour	old, stale consignment
CAU3	too little raising agent	someone forgot to add it
CAU4	too much sugar	nozzle flowing freely
CAU5	too much cocoa	hopper faulty
CAU6	too little cocoa	hopper faulty
CAU7	faulty cocoa	change of source
CAU8	wrong sugar	faulty batch
CAU9	not enough air in mixture	dust cover blocked
CAU10	not enough air in mixture	fan slow or stopped
CAU11	oven too cool	gases too cool
CAU12	factory too warm	warm temperature outside
CAU13	oven too hot	gas temperature too high
CAU14	oven too hot	cooling failed
CAU15	too little sugar	nozzle opening restricted
CAU16	faulty flour	faulty batch
CAU17	rancid butter	warm temperature outside
CAU18	faulty cocoa	faulty batch
CAU19	oven too cool	low temperature gases

Table 5.4 The fault-test rules: ⟨*fault*⟩ CONFIRMED BY ⟨*test*⟩

Rule number	Fault	Test
CON1	dust cover blocked	remove back from dust cover and look
CON2	fan slow or stopped	shine strobe light and the steady, black line is not visible
CON3	faulty batch	send sample to laboratory
CON4	warm day	take reading from wall thermometer – should be less than 80°
CON5	hopper faulty	measure time for level in hopper to drop by one graduation – should be 4 minutes
CON6	change of source	check bags
CON7	old consignment	check date on bags
CON8	someone forgot	check log *or* ask supervisor
CON9	nozzle flowing freely	see if sugar flowing steadily from nozzle, without breaking into droplets
CON10	nozzle opening restricted	see if sugar dripping at less than 10 drops per minute
CON11	cooling failed	tap turned on *and* water jacket cool to touch *and* pump not vibrating
CON12	cooling failed	tap turned on *and* water jacket warm to touch
CON13	gas temperature too high	white colour at viewing window
CON14	low temperature gases	black colour at viewing window
CON15	low temperature gases	red colour at viewing window
CON16	low temperature gases	flickering light at viewing window

might be difficult to elicit from the old hands who feel they have nothing to learn from a computer and, besides, they 'do it all by feel' anyway. Such obstacles require patience and tact to overcome. Observing the expert at work, if possible, might suggest what some of the problem solving strategies are.

Assuming the knowledge elicitation proceeds successfully, the knowledge engineer could end up with four sets of rules which look like Tables 5.2, 5.3, 5.4 and 5.5.

5.4 Inference

As explained in the introduction, this chapter will illustrate some of the important concepts of expert systems with the help of

Table 5.5 The fault-action rules: IF ⟨*fault*⟩ THEN DO ⟨*action*⟩

Rule number	Fault	Action	Lost production
ITD1	dust cover blocked	clean and replace dust cover	some
ITD2	fan slow or stopped	call fitter	major
ITD3	*suspected* faulty batch	report fault to supervisor	major
ITD4	warm day	report fault to supervisor	some
		IF butter rancid THEN discard batch	major
ITD5	hopper faulty	call fitter	major
ITD6	old consignment *or* change of source	report fault *and* discard batch *and* *check* faulty batch	major
ITD7	someone forgot	add ingredient *and* report fault *and* discard batch	major
ITD8	nozzle flowing freely	turn down sugar supply	some
ITD9	nozzle opening restricted	switch off sugar supply *and* remove nozzle *and* replace with spare *and* send faulty nozzle for cleaning	some
ITD10	cooling failed *and* water jacked warm to touch	call fitter	major
ITD11	cooling failed *and* pump not vibrating	call electrician	major
ITD12	cooling failed *and* water tap turned off	turn on tap	some
ITD13	gas temperature too high	turn down oxygen input	some
ITD14	low temperature gases *and* black colour	restart override	some
ITD15	low temperature gases *and* flickering light	raise alarm *and* evacuate factory	factory shutdown
ITD16	low temperature gases *and* red colour	turn up oxygen supply	some

examples. In this section, we shall consider forward and backward chaining.

To understand properly these examples, the reader is urged to refer to the tables and diagrams that accompany this chapter. As data are acquired and rules fired within the expert system, facts will be stored in the expert system's Working Memory. The contents of the Working Memory will be displayed in boxes:

> Contents of Working Memory

The source of each fact will also be displayed, in most cases the name of the rule which fired giving that fact as its consequent.

5.5 Forward chaining— example 1

As an example of how forward chaining may be applied, let us suppose that an operator sees that the chocolate is bubbling.

> Trigger: chocolate bubbling

Reasoning forwards, we use Rule ITS13 to suggest the hypothesis 'oven too hot'

Trigger:	chocolate bubbling
ITS13:	oven too hot

Scanning on down the list of ITS rules, we see that there are no others with 'chocolate bubbling' as the antecedent. So, this is the only hypothesis. Turning to Rule CAU13, this suggests the likely fault as 'gas temperature too high'.

Trigger:	chocolate is bubbling
ITS13:	oven too hot
CAU13:	gas temperature too high

Rule CAU14 also has 'oven too hot' as the antecedent, so we add 'cooling failed' to the list of possible faults.

Trigger:	chocolate bubbling
ITS13:	oven too hot
CAU13:	gas temperature too high
CAU14:	cooling failed

Next, the faults must be tested. Rule CON13 suggests a test for 'gas temperature too high', ie that there is a white colour at the viewing window.

Trigger:	chocolate is bubbling
ITS13:	oven too hot
CAU13:	gas temperature too high
CAU14:	cooling failed
CON13:	white colour at viewing window

Suppose that the operator goes to check this and sees that the gas colour is perfectly normal, as an orangey glow. That rules out 'gas temperature too high' as a fault, but 'cooling failed' still needs to be checked. So, the failed test and the fault that suggested it should be marked as deleted from the working memory.

Trigger:	chocolate is bubbling	
ITS13:	oven too hot	
CAU13:	gas temperature too high	X
CAU14:	cooling failed	
CON13:	white colour at viewing window	X

Two tests exist to check whether the cooling has failed, supplied by Rules CON11 and CON12, because there are different ways in which the cooling could fail

Trigger:	chocolate bubbling	
ITS13:	oven too hot	
CAU13:	gas temperature too high	X
CAU14:	cooling failed	
CON13:	white colour at viewing window	X
CON11:	tap turned on *and* water	
CON12:	jacket cool to touch *and*	
	pump not vibrating	
	tap turned on *and*	
	water jacket warm to touch	

This is reflected in the actions that are recommended by Rules ITD10, ITD11 and ITD12. The operator is requested by the expert system to check several items and depending on the answers given, the system can infer the particular fault and recommend the appropriate action (*see* Figure 5.2).

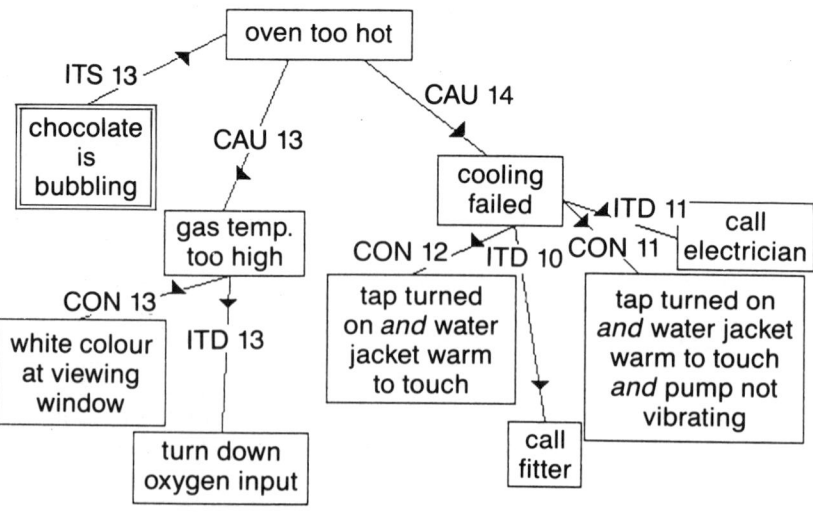

Figure 5.2 Forward chaining

Starting with the trigger 'chocolate is bubbling', the expert system can reason forwards, using the indicated rules.

In this example, the reasoning proceeds forwards from antecedent to consequent each time. The control strategy of the inference engine had to cope with the possibility of two faults (which could have occurred simultaneously) and be able to recommend tests for the second fault once the first one had been discounted.

5.6 Backward chaining— example 2

Forward chaining in example 1 can produce something like expert behaviour quite well, but it is rather rigid. The reasoning process must always start with the trigger and go forwards. Figure 5.1 shows which parts of the inference process are carried out within the expert system itself and which are concerned with the triggers, tests and presentation of conclusions. If the inference process began at some point denoted in Figure 5.1 as being inside the expert system, then forward reasoning would not let us infer which triggers would be manifest, since that would require reasoning from consequent to antecedent. That would be backward chaining.

To illustrate the usefulness of backward chaining, let us consider another example (*see* Figure 5.3). Suppose on the way to work one day, one of the operators notices that the weather is unusually warm. This suggests to the alert person that some faults could probably occur because of the heat and that it might be worth

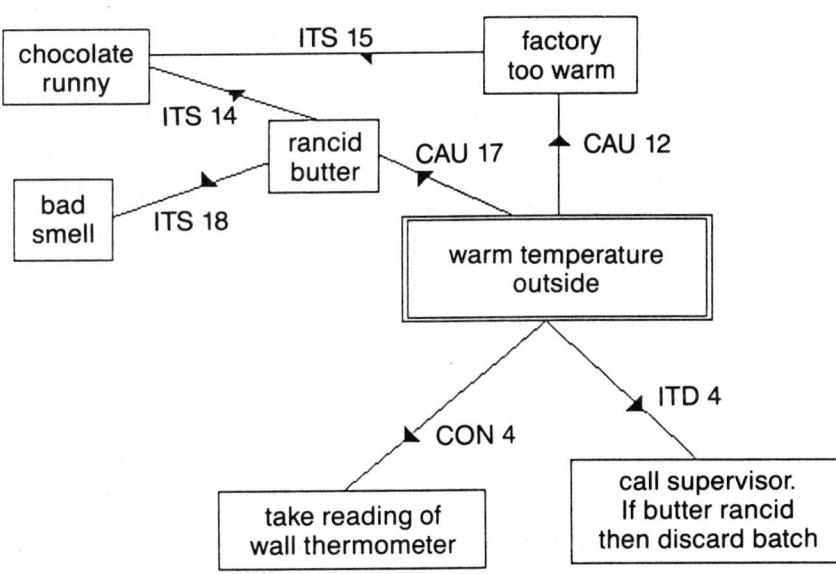

Figure 5.3 Forwards and backwards chaining

Starting with 'warm temperature outside', the expert system can reason forwards using rules CON4 and ITD4. Rules CAU17 and CAU12 can be used to start backward chaining to reach the triggers 'chocolate runny' and 'bad smell'.

consulting the expert system to find out what to watch out for. 'Warm day' is one of the faults that the system recognises.

```
Fault:    warm day
```

Rule ITD4 reasons forward to recommend that the shift supervisor should be advised and the batch discarded if the butter is rancid. This could lead to a major production loss, so it would be a fault worth avoiding if possible.

```
Fault:    warm day
ITD4:     discard batch
```

Rules CAU12 and CAU17 have 'warm day' as their consequents, so reasoning backwards suggests the hypotheses 'factory too warm' and 'rancid butter'.

```
Fault:    warm day
ITD4:     discard batch
CAU12:    factory too warm   B
CAU17:    rancid butter   B
```

Reasoning backwards with the ITS rules reveals that the triggers are 'chocolate runny' (ITS14 and ITS15) and 'bad smell' (ITS18). So the operator is forewarned to watch out for the chocolate becoming runny or a bad smell developing.

```
Fault:    warm day
ITD4:     discard batch
CAU12:    factory too warm   B
CAU17:    rancid butter   B
ITS14:    chocolate runny
ITS15:    chocolate runny
ITS18:    bad smell
```

Incidentally, reasoning forward with the rule CON4 suggests the test of taking the reading on the wall thermometer. So, the operator has an extra piece of information and can keep an eye on the thermometer as well.

By volunteering the information that the weather is warm and using a mixture of forward and backward reasoning, the user of the expert system is able to discover the seriousness of a developing fault and finding out the triggers and tests which should be monitored during the day.

5.7 Control strategy

We have already seen a simple example where more than one fault could occur. In the simplest case, the expert system chooses to test the faults in the order in which the rules suggest them, but this could lead to problems. If the biscuits are burnt, rules ITS3, ITS4 and ITS5 all suggest possible hypotheses. Each of these hypotheses generates possible faults that would need to be tested before the true cause or causes could be discovered. When many hypotheses are suggested, it would seem to be a good idea to assign some sort of priority to the test procedures.

There are many candidate criteria which could be used for determining priority. In this simple case, the expert system has used the potential production loss associated with each fault. It would seem a good idea to rank the possible faults according to the amount of product that would be lost, taking care to identify the most expensive faults as quickly as possible, so as to minimise the production loss.

Other possible criteria that a more sophisticated control strategy could take into account are:

– probability of the fault occurring;
– cost of performing the test;
– potential damage that the fault could inflict;
– if more than one trigger is observed, whether the fault is suggested by more than one hypothesis.

If several faults were suggested, the human expert would presumably be prudent in performing tests to check the most common faults before proceeding to check the least likely. Similarly, if a test is difficult or expensive to perform, then that would be left until later as well. The interplay of these criteria might be quite complex in certain situations, and it might be the case that another expert system could be used to order the tests. Such a 'meta expert system' might contain rules like:

IF none of the faults have a probability of occurrence of more than 10 per cent
THEN test them in order of possible damage.

5.8 Other enhancements

This section discusses some further points raised within the case study, concerning user interfaces, knowledge representation and other topics. Two more examples are included.

Costing the faults

The above section on control strategy points out the importance of having a sensible way of deciding in which order to check the faults. The rule formats as originally presented in Table 5.1 did not have any knowledge associated with them that would enable a control strategy to operate in this way. As new facts were gathered, they were added to the working memory, so the only control the expert system builder would have over the order in which tests occurred would be to order carefully the rules as they appeared within Tables 5.2–5.5. In this way, by placing the most damaging faults at the top of the table, they would appear first in the list of tests that need to be carried out. This kind of solution is unsatisfactory, because the criteria for deciding in which order the tests should be applied are not directly available to the expert system. They would have to be written down elsewhere in an accompanying manual, making the system unwieldy and difficult to maintain when new rules are to be added or other changes become necessary.

A better way to do this is to extend the knowledge representation format so that the extra item of information may be included. Of course, the inference engine would also need to be able to make proper use of any such additional items, via its control strategy. Extending the knowledge representation format means that the extra knowledge is explicit and is there to be checked and amended if necessary.

and and *or* Operators

Several of the rules contain *and* and *or* operators, eg CON11, CON12, ITD6, ITD7 and ITD11. These operators serve many different purposes.

In rules CON11, CON12, ITD6, ITD7 and ITD9, for example, *and* appears in the consequent of the rules. For both CON and ITD rule types, the consequents are procedures that must be carried out by the expert system user. So, the *and* serves to group together the separate items of the procedure.

When *and* appears in the antecedent of the rule, as in ITD10, ITD11 and others, its function is different. Here, *and* means that all the conditions must be true before the rule is fired. For ITD10, this means that 'cooling failed' must be true and 'water jacket warm to touch' must be true at the same time before the consequent to that rule ('call fitter') can be added to Working Memory.

There is one example in the tables of *or* appearing as part of the consequent of a rule, in CON8. In order to confirm the fault 'someone forgot', the user is asked to 'check log' *or* 'ask supervisor'. Here, the user is given some discretion as to which action to carry out. It may happen that the user carries out both actions – this is not an *exclusive or*.

Rule ITD6 contains an example of an *or* appearing in the antecedent of a rule. Here, if either condition is true, the rule will fire and the consequent will be added to Working Memory. This use of *or* has the convenient property of cutting down the number of rules, since without this use of *or*, two rules would be needed to convey the same information:

> ITD6a IF old consignment THEN DO report fault *and* discard batch *and* check faulty batch.
> ITD6b IF change of source THEN DO report fault *and* discard batch *and* check faulty batch.

This use of *or* has not been fully exploited in this case study, for simplicity, but there are many examples in Tables 5.2 and 5.3 where it could be used.

Other embedded operators

Rule ITD6 contains an instruction to '*check* faulty batch'. Although the fault has been identified, the rule has this extra addendum which adds 'faulty batch' to the list of possible faults in Working Memory. This fault fires CON3 which requires sending a sample to the laboratory for tests. However, sending material to the laboratory can mean a long wait for the result of the test. All the other tests can be performed by the operator and the results obtained fairly quickly. There often is not time to await results from the laboratory, so ITD3 has the rider 'Suspected' attached to the antecedent. Before obtaining the test results, the operator should proceed with the action recommended.

Rule ITD4 has another kind of extension to the Knowledge Representation format. The consequent to the rule contains an IF . . . THEN clause.

ITD4	warm day	report fault to supervisor	some
		IF butter rancid THEN discard	major
		batch	

This clause is directed to the operator as part of the test, so it does not directly affect the expert system, since it does not add anything to Working Memory. However, if the Control Strategy were to use the potential lost production to assign priority to tests, then a rule containing such a clause would require special attention.

5.9 Factory safety – example 3

This carefully elicited and refined knowledge can be put to other uses too. The most expensive fault is shown at ITD15, when low temperature gases are suspected and a flickering light is observed at the viewing window. In these cases, the alarm must be raised and the factory evacuated (*see* Figure 5.4).

| Action: | evacuate factory |

Reasoning backwards, we find that low temperature gases are suspected by the hypotheses 'oven too cool'.

Action:	evacuate factory
ITD15:	low temperature gases
	and flickering light B
CAU19:	oven too cool B

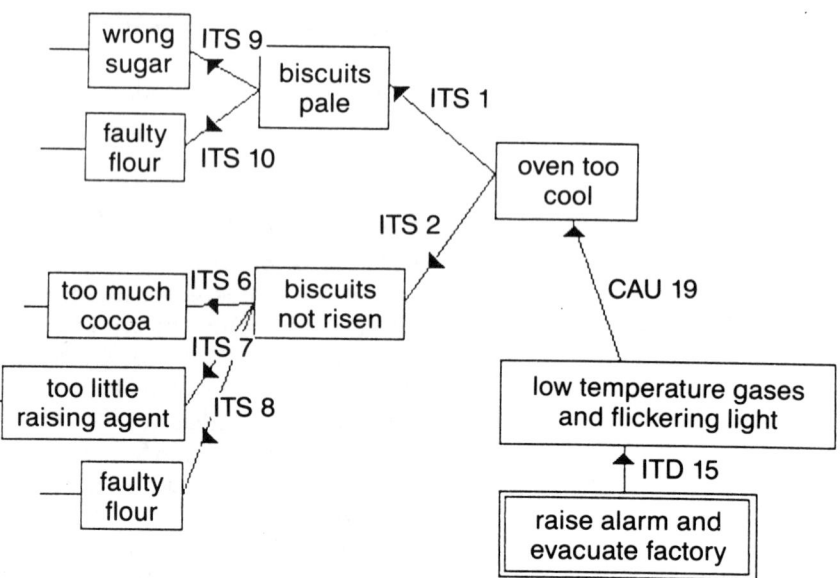

Figure 5.4 Factory safety

From the action 'raise alarm and evacuate factory', the expert system could reason backwards to find which triggers might eventually lead to this action.

This hypothesis is suggested by the triggers 'biscuits not risen' or 'biscuits too pale', reasoning backwards with ITS1 and ITS2.

Action:	evacuate factory
ITD15:	low temperature gases *and* flickering light B
CAU19:	oven too cool B
ITS1:	biscuits pale B
ITS2:	biscuits not risen B

However, these triggers suggest many other hypotheses as well, as can be seen by reasoning *forwards* from ITS6, ITS7, ITS8, ITS9 and ITS10.

Action:	evacuate factory
ITD15:	low temperature gases *and* flickering light B
CAU19:	oven too cool B
ITS1:	biscuits pale B
ITS2:	biscuits not risen B
ITS6:	too much cocoa
ITS7:	too little raising agent
ITS8:	faulty flour
ITS9:	wrong sugar
ITS10:	faulty flour

If these triggers were seen, without a good control strategy, time would be wasted searching relatively trivial hypotheses. Apart from using a better control strategy, the factory managers could decide that since they now know that this is the only test for an expensive fault, it should be changed from the status of *test* to *trigger*, ie something which captures the operator's attention immediately. This could be done by implementing some sort of automatic alarm system which would be sprung immediately the temperature began to drop, so that the conditions on the other side of the viewing window could be monitored more carefully.

It is worth noting that triggers and tests are the two classes of object where the expert system has access to the outside world. As we have seen, tests incur a cost, but triggers have no cost associated with them, because they come to the operator's attention as a matter of course. Hence, triggers are no more than zero-cost tests. That is why it is not too difficult conceptually to change a test into a trigger.

Furthermore, it can be seen that sending material to the laboratory for tests occurs quite frequently, suggesting that the time for receipt of results could be cut. Faulty ingredients are deemed responsible under rules CAU1, CAU2, CAU7, CAU8, CAU16 and CAU18. ITD6 suggests it too. This is particularly important because so many triggers could be due to faulty materials that it is worth doing lab checks as a matter of course, perhaps regularly sampling the ingredients of the biscuits.

5.10 Generating explanations

At the start of this case study, it was mentioned that one of the purposes of introducing an expert system was to help train the workforce and the rule-based knowledge representation format was chosen so that explanations could easily be generated. So far, we have not indicated how this could be done. The Working Memory is very useful for this purpose.

Let us look back to the contents of the Working Memory at one point during example 1.

Trigger:	chocolate bubbling
ITS13:	oven too hot
CAU13:	gas temperature too high
CAU14:	cooling failed

This may be used to generate a fairly rudimentary explanation of the expert system's reasoning as follows. Remember, that at this point, the operator has supplied the trigger and is awaiting the outcome. Another program will be required to generate explanations, also with access to the Working Memory and rule base (*see* Figure 5.5). There are various ways in which the explanation could be presented to the user, but we shall consider a simple method which uses so-called 'canned text'.

From the contents of Working Memory, the explanation generator picks up the word 'Trigger'. From the canned text, it

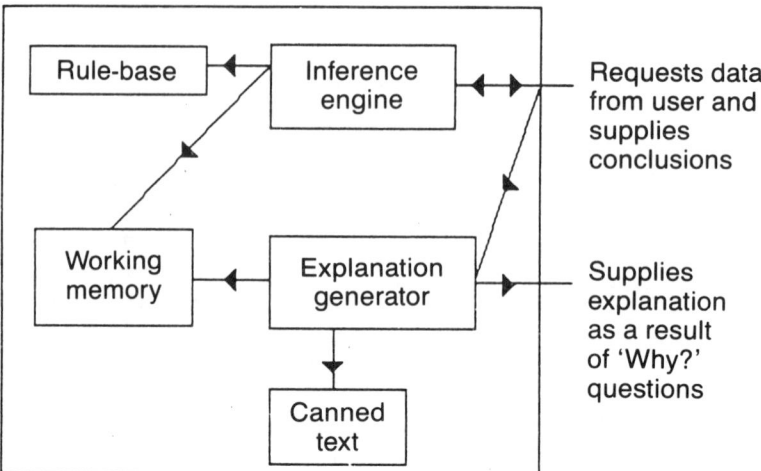

Figure 5.5 An explanation generator

During the consultation, the inference engine requests data and provides conclusions. When the user asks a 'Why?' question, the explanation generator takes over temporarily using Working Memory and its own canned text to generate a response.

produces a phrase which may be combined with the actual trigger to produce the sentence: *The operator observed the trigger: chocolate bubbling.* The next line contains a rule number, with the rule's consequent, so a little more canned text would help generate: *From this I conclude oven too hot.* The Working Memory contains two CAU consequents, so a more complex sentence could be required: *This could be caused by gas temperature too high or cooling failed.*

The next stage in the inference process was:

Trigger:	chocolate is bubbling
ITS13:	oven too hot
CAU13:	gas temperature too high
CAU14:	cooling failed
CON13:	white colour at viewing window

There is no explicit connection now between the test now presented, 'white colour at viewing window', and the two suggested faults. However, the explanation generator has two possible ways of finding this out. The simpler is to rely on the ordering of the contents of Working Memory and assume that this test refers to the first fault listed. The other way would be to use the reference to CON13 to quickly check the rule base and obtain the rule's antecedent. So, another sentence could be generated reading: *Gas temperature too high may be confirmed by testing white colour at viewing window.*

Recall that in the example, this test failed, ruling out 'gas temperature too high' as a possible fault. Rather than deleting all references to this from Working Memory, the two relevant entries in Working Memory were marked with X instead. The reason for that should now be apparent. It is important that the explanation generator should have access to past actions when it is asked to provide explanations. Had those entries been deleted, and the explanation generator asked later to explain what was going on, it would have had no access to that information.

If the explanation generator relies solely on the ordering of the rules to link antecedents and consequents, it would be sorely confused by the introduction of backward chaining. This is why backward chained entries were marked with B. As the expert system embarks on mixed inference, with both forward and backward chaining, so the explanation generator is going to need to access the rule base to be sure that it is linking items correctly. Additionally, its job could be made easier at the expense of the inference engine, by extending the contents of Working Memory to record which entry in Working Memory fired the rule, whether backwards or forwards.

The simple explanations outlined above could easily be improved. The canned text is little more than a more acceptable expansion of the rule formats of Table 5.1. The readability of the explanations could be further improved if the triggers, hypotheses, faults etc were also rendered in a more English-like or verbose style. References to the rule numbers could be included too, but they are more likely to be of interest to the knowledge engineer or expert system builder than the day-to-day user.

The presentation of explanations is an important part of designing an expert system. Different levels of explanation might be required for different users, with an option to request more information as the user starts to query the system. It might also be worth including a facility to enable the user to enter comments or notes, indicating failures of the rules, possible or actual exceptions, new rules etc.

The informativeness of explanations is limited by the knowledge in the knowledge base. Deeper questions about why a white colour at the viewing window indicates that the gas temperature is too high cannot be answered with the knowledge base of this case study, since no more than the known observations are recorded. Knowledge of this nature may well exist, but it is likely to reside in the minds of the experts and possibly in process manuals.

The explanations described so far use the contents of Working Memory to explain the chains of reasoning, under forward and backward chaining. But another part of the expert system is influencing the way in which the expert system presents its results to the waiting world outside – the control strategy. Recall that this is assigning priorities to the tests which the user must carry out. We leave it to the reader's imagination to outline how that might be accomplished.

Good explanations are very important. The design of a good explanations generator is not necessarily a trivial task. It involves building prototypes, letting the users try them and being as accommodating as possible, within the limits of the knowledge available to the system.

5.11 Concluding remarks

We have attempted to introduce some of the basic techniques of knowledge representation and inference in expert systems through a fictitious case study on the Chocolate Biscuit Factory. Several important features of expert systems have become apparent.

Once some knowledge about the domain has been acquired, it is quickly clear that many things can be done with it. Forward chaining alone soon becomes restrictive and backward chaining is added to utilise the knowledge more effectively. Then, we need to extend the rule-based knowledge representation format to allow special cases to be included and to take account of practical limitations, such as the time delay in getting the results from a laboratory test.

Then a sensible control strategy is needed so that the faults can be tested in an efficient order, which means having some more knowledge about other properties of the faults and tests, such as their probabilities, costs and potential consequences. With a control strategy, the expert system is beginning to acquire something like a mind of its own, so explanations become all the more important. This opens up another range of possibilities, because the knowledge available to the expert system is the only thing that limits the information content in the explanations, and it is always possible to add more knowledge, extending the knowledge representation format as need be.

Expert system shells are not usually flexible enough to provide these development ideas. It can let the willing user of expert systems get started, but more and more possibilities will suggest themselves.

5.12 Appendix – table of objects

Triggers	Hypotheses
biscuits pale	oven too cool
biscuits not risen	too much cocoa
biscuits burnt	too much sugar
chocolate sticky	oven too hot
chocolate bubbling	too little raising agent
chocolate runny	faulty flour
chocolate too dark	not enough air in mixture
chocolate too light	faulty cocoa
bad smell	rancid butter
	factory too warm
	wrong sugar

Faults

change of source
old, stale consignment
someone forgot to add it
nozzle flowing freely
hopper faulty
faulty batch
dust cover blocked
fan slow or stopped
gases too cool
warm day
gas temperature too high
cooling failed
nozzle opening restricted
low temperature gases

Actions

clean and replace dust cover
call fitter
report fault to supervisor
discard batch
add ingredient
turn down sugar supply
switch off sugar supply
remove nozzle *and* replace with
    spare
send faulty nozzle for cleaning
call electrician
turn on tap
turn down oxygen input
restart override
raise alarm
evacuate factory
turn up oxygen supply

Tests

remove back from dust cover and look
shine strobe light and the steady, black line is not visible
send sample to laboratory
take readings of wall thermometer – should be less than 80°
measure time for level in hopper to drop by one graduation – should be 4
    minutes
check bags
check date on bags
check log
ask supervisor
see if sugar flowing steadily from nozzle without breaking into droplets
see if sugar dripping at less than 10 drops per minute
tap turned on *and* water jacket cool to touch *and* pump not vibrating
tap turned on *and* water jacket warm to touch
white colour at viewing window
black colour at viewing window
red colour at viewing window
flickering light at viewing window

Chapter 6 Interfacing the expert system to the outside world

6.1 Introduction

The earliest expert systems acquired all their data about the world outside by communicating with a user via a screen and keyboard. There was no integration with sensors or other programs and the expert system interface paid very scant attention to the needs of the user. It was hardly surprising that even interested and supportive users found expert systems difficult and unwieldy. However, over the last ten years expert systems are being designed to fit into their environments, rather than trying to force the environment to change to accommodate them.

This is often the case with new computer applications. The first prototypes are written by technical wizards who love the system for itself and don't mind difficult communications. As the technical knowledge of these systems accumulates, the original technical program can be programmed more efficiently and diminishes in size, but improves in effectiveness, and can be programmed to be more compact and run more efficiently. At that point, the technique can be introduced to the wide world of users, who are not enamoured by the program itself, and demand that it should be easy to use and accommodate to their world. So, the original laboratory program, which spent 10 per cent or less of its code on user interface, becomes unrecognisable with 90 per cent of the total code devoted to user interface.

The early expert systems concentrated on the facilities of the inference engine and the styles of knowledge representation that needed to be provided. There was grudging attention paid to the needs of the user, because they were after all the expert system's communications device, providing data, carrying out actions and generally serving the expert system. Expert systems were programmed as stand-alone devices, with little or no communication with other software packages. The systems were so slow, since there was no need to operate at a speed above that of the human input device, so that acquiring data automatically from sensors was not a consideration.

However, all that has changed now. Expert systems will not be accepted within organisations if they are unpleasing and difficult to use, no matter the quality of their functionality. Real-time systems are available now and promise more for the future.

This chapter will describe some of the developments in interfacing to the user and sensors, pointing how expert systems can be tailored to present and future needs.

6.2 Communicating with the user

As mentioned above, the original expert systems concentrated on the technical issues involved in designing the knowledge representation and inference engines. Now that the technical community is more accustomed to the idea of expert systems, the problem is how to design the team, consisting of the human and the computer. Whereas before the expert system was expected to control the dialogue, now it is expected that the user will be able to take control when required or restore control to the machine. Furthermore, the whole distribution of work between human and machine can be re-thought, given that the computer would be able to access other programs and devices.

Most of the guidelines for user interface design still apply when designing expert systems, since in many respects they are no different from other computer programs. Rather than repeating the standard advice, we shall try to concentrate on those aspects of expert systems where their use might require more thought (*see* Table 6.1).

Table 6.1 Comparison of expert systems with other software tools

Fault diagnosis expert systems	Financial spreadsheet
Short consultations	Extended work sessions
High speed trouble-shooting mode	Only one mode
Support user-paced training and query	What-if queries
Shared dialogue control	User controls dialogue
Knowledge acquisition and prototyping	Model construction and testing
Process control expert system	**Financial spreadsheet**
Controlled testing possible	Controlled testing difficult
Operates within bounded environment	Operates within complex environment
Might only need limited supervision	Does not run automatically
Designed for use by operators with limited specialised training	Designed for use by trained professionals

6.3 Dialogue control

The first advisory expert systems allowed the user little control over the progress of the consultation, perhaps a little too like interacting with the original oracle-like expert. The expert system requested information from the user, who responded by typing answers at the keyboard. The user could temporarily interrupt the consultation by asking 'Why?' questions, whereupon the expert system would dump a trace of the rules it had already fired and those hypotheses it was about to test. Bewilderingly, this could include the blind alleys that had already failed. Other canned text could also be presented. Then the expert system would resume the consultation at the point the interruption had occurred. The user had no control over the path of the consultation and could not short-cut any of the question and answering, even if some of the information had already been supplied earlier. The user could not volunteer information that he/she thought might be important and could not help the expert system focus its enquiries. The questions were sometimes inappropriate to the domain and the user's style of inference and level of understanding, having been designed to satisfy the inference engine and knowledge representation. Remember too that in those early days it was believed that a single expert system shell would work in any domain and when the right shell was found, it would displace all the others.

In other words, the expert system treated the user as a dumb communications medium and totally ignored the user's own experience and knowledge. It is hardly surprising that these expert systems failed to be accepted and had to change.

There is no inherent reason why expert systems should adopt such a superior attitude. There are many styles of interacting with experts; so let it be with expert systems.

Trouble-shooting style   When a fault occurs, the expert system must identify the fault as quickly as possible. Under fault conditions, many data signals are available to the operators, possibly with alarms and warning signals ringing or flashing, increasing the operators' sense of panic and impairing their ability to reason clearly. Under these abnormal conditions, expert systems can be a godsend. Their ability to reason consistently is crucial, but they must also be able to respond to the situation, requiring the minimum amount of information from the users and recommending safety actions as quickly as possible, perhaps even before the correct fault has been definitely located.

Critiquing style   Once the crisis has passed, the user might want to sit down with the expert system for an extended work session, querying the expert system on why it recommended certain actions and why it favoured one diagnosis over another plausible one. The user might want to present an alternative diagnosis of the fault to the expert system and have the system compare the suggested diagnosis with its own diagnosis and the real fault, if known and different from the other two. At this stage, the user and expert system should be able to critique each other's performance, pointing out areas of the plant where one diagnosis might have been favoured over another. This style of interaction is commonly observed when people consult a human expert. It is important for training new experts and encouraging people to accept the expert's advice.

6.4 Style of interaction

Historically, expert systems required the user to interact with the expert system by reading material written on a screen and responding by typing at a keyboard. There is no reason why this should continue to be the case. Experience with using expert systems shows that not everyone is comfortable typing their answers and text alone is not an adequate means of communicating information to users.

The style of interaction should be determined predominantly by the users. In some examples, the users have been closely involved in the design of the interface, which helps to ensure their acceptance of the system. If users are unable to participate in the actual design, their needs should be assessed thoroughly and the interface designed accordingly. Special keyboards can be specified, for example, or screen-based interfaces, with mice, icons, windows and pointers.

In many process control applications, text-based output is a minor part of the information requirements of the operators. To monitor the process, the operators need trend displays, indication of tolerance limits, colour coding and facilities such as viewing historical information, status queries etc. The fact that an expert system underlies the display might not be important for 90 per cent of their day's work (*see* Chapter 8 for further discussion of these points).

There is a strong case to be made for believing that real-time applications of expert systems should always give the operator control over the expert system's action. In safety-critical applications, the operator remains responsible for the safe operation of the plant. Furthermore, the operator needs to retain some skill in the operation of the plant, so that he/she can take over should the automatic equipment fail. The necessary level of skill is unlikely to be supported if the operator relinquishes all responsibility to the machine.

What should be done when an emergency occurs can be a problem, though. If the machine takes over because things are happening too fast for the human to keep up, and the machine makes a mistake, who is to blame? Or, if the human takes control, and ignores or contradicts the advice of the machine, whose fault is the disaster then? These are knotty questions. Regarding the expert system as another piece of automatic equipment, and designing it in that way, is probably a more fruitful approach to a solution than looking on it as an expert in a box.

6.5 Explanation

The favoured method of explanation is to construct a trace of the rules triggered so far. This method can be useful if handled sympathetically, by programmer and expert system user alike. It is also best confined to systems that use only short chains of reasoning. In other situations, where the inference process is more complex or the users less well acquainted with the domain, a rule-trace explanation might serve to frighten and confuse rather than enlighten.

Explanations can be supported with other Help facilities, such as prepared paragraphs of text that can explain background to the application, such as variable names, methods of inference etc.

Text-based explanations have their role, but any computer system that appears to use English well can create the misleading impression that it has a commensurate level of intelligence. The user might find it frustrating to obtain well expressed summaries of knowledge and information if the machine cannot be made to understand exactly what the user wants to know about.

Research is proceeding in several directions to try to improve this state of affairs.

Natural language understanding   Instead of responding from a menu of choices or using one of a set of commands, the user types in a query in natural English. The expert system responds with an explanation at an appropriate level of detail.

Deep modelling   The expert system understands the domain more thoroughly, with 'deep' knowledge about the equipment and processes which are involved. The expert system's inference processes would be based on first principles, and could therefore be made more intelligible to the user, since this is similar to knowledge that a reasonably well-informed user might have. Appropriate levels of detail in the explanation would also be required.

User modelling   The expert system maintains a knowledge base on each user, with a record of the kinds of things that each user knows about and is expert in. The expert system could tailor the explanations by short-cutting or summarising those areas the expert knows about and providing detail to match the user's expertise and areas of interest.

Intelligent front ends   Intelligent front ends (IFEs) are programs which sit between the user and perhaps a group of other programs, on statistical analysis, for example. The IFE knows about the domain of statistics and can help the user select the correct statistics program for their data. Instead of modelling the user, the IFE concentrates on the intricacies of the domain.

Better knowledge representations   This approach is based on the belief that better natural language explanations will be based on better representations of the knowledge, which are more akin to the way users express and understand knowledge. Better representations would have the benefit of supporting better explanations as well as easier knowledge acquisition.

Text-based explanations are not the only form of explanation that is possible, however. In many process control domains, diagrams of flows and component states are the more natural means of communication between users, and between user and expert system. Hence, graphical displays are likely to be very important, both in displaying on-line data and for explaining reasoning.

The need for explanations depends on the users and the domain, and also on the level of acceptance of the expert system. During the phases of developing the expert system, testing and acceptance by the users, explanations would be very important for increasing the users' confidence in the expert system's conclusions. However, once it has been accepted into working practice, the need for explanation facilities is likely to diminish.

6.6 Communicating with sensors

Few real-time process control expert systems have been constructed so far, but *see* Chapter 8 for an extensive case study. This section will review the requirements for a real-time expert system, as distinct from other real-time systems and advisory expert systems. The related research area of intelligent robots will be discussed to see what lessons may be learned from efforts there to integrate data from many sensors and take decisions in real time. Finally, we shall review briefly some existing real-time expert systems which have been reported in the literature.

Requirements for real-time expert systems

Throughout this book, we have maintained a distinction between advisory and controlling expert systems. Advisory expert systems are used to provide advice and normally rely on screen-based communication with the user. A controlling expert system acquires data automatically and either carries out control actions autonomnously, or reports to the user who might carry out the action or grant authorisation to the system. Heuristic techniques play a role in both kinds of system; controlling systems use heuristic information to interpret directly sensor data and advisory systems apply heuristic judgements to take decisions about interpretations provided either by analytic or heuristic methods.

There are two main requirements of any real-time system that we should mention briefly at the outset, since they will strongly influence how the other system requirements are met:

Timeliness of response   Under dynamically changing conditions, the controller must generate a control action quickly enough for the desired effect to occur.

Interruptibility   When abnormal situations occur, the system must be able to use alarm signals efficiently to recommend recovery actions, subject to requirement above, while maintaining efficient control elsewhere.

Turning to the specifics of expert systems, their performance would be affected in the following ways:

Sensor validation   Faults occur in sensors as well as in the other components of the plant and the materials flowing through it. A deviant reading could be due to either a genuine fault on the plant or a faulty reading from a sensor. Sensor readings could be checked by comparing with related sensors, performing a small experiment on the plant or requesting a maintenance engineer to check the suspect device.

Hypothesis and belief maintenance   The expert system must try to maintain a complete and consistent set of beliefs about itself and its world, ie the plant. The system will use inconsistent and time-dependent data, so must be able to review its beliefs as more data become available.

Remembering and forgetting   The system would need to realise that data become out of date and need to be deleted when no longer required. Believed assertions might have to be replaced as measurements or other more certain assertions come available. The time difference between when an assertion was made and when it is used to perform inference could make that assertion at worst wrong, but at least suspect or irrelevant. The system would need to know which facts and assertions are worth remembering and which should be forgotten.

Knowledge maintenance   The process plant will be changed during its lifetime, as components are replaced, portions of the plant closed down and new parts and processes added. The knowledge base must adapt too as these changes are made, so as to maintain its usefulness. New process knowledge is likely to be acquired too and that has to be accommodated as well. The knowledge base would need to be partitioned into separate areas so as to enable maintenance, but also to take advantage of different knowledge representation formats, levels of detail and knowledge types.

While these are difficult and demanding requirements, there are some ways in which real-time process control expert systems have advantages over other advisory systems.

Modelling and simulation   Many processes have already been studied in some depth before the advent of expert systems and have more or less adequate simulation models available. These can be used to iron out the worst of the expert system's wrinkles and can be useful for designing the user interface. Advisory expert systems have to rely on recorded cases, but using these for testing can produce an expert system which is too closely tuned to what it has already encountered. Simulation can be used to generate a large number of fictional cases.

Recommendation   Once some early confidence has been gained in the expert system's behaviour it may be introduced to the process, but remain in open loop, that is it may acquire data, perform inferences, reach conclusions and recommend actions, but without carrying out any direct actions on the plant. Its suggestions could be critiqued by the operators until it appeared to be within a specified range of the operators' chosen actions. One should recall that the operators themselves are unlikely to be acting optimally, so it might not be wise to match the expert system completely to their behaviour.

Repeated testing   As with modelling and simulation, an on-line expert system is required to exercise continuously its decision-making processes. Its performance can therefore be monitored and assessed. If the system explains how it reaches its conclusions, for example by indicating which rules it fires, then faults in the rules or inference processes can be spotted and corrected.

Modularity   With a well-partitioned knowledge base, it is possible to install the expert system one piece at a time. In this way, the technology and user reaction can both be tested and improved.

Intelligent robots

Intelligent robots have many similarities with process control systems. They both need to integrate data from many sources and take decisions in real time. They need to be able to avert damage, whether from a faulty process or an approaching object. Their sensors are noisy and not always reliable and they may both be involved in the manipulation of hazardous material.

The differences include the fact that process plant remains fixed in one place, whereas the robot could be moving around in an unfamiliar environment. Robots would like to carry their processing power around with them, which further constrains the resource requirements, since physical bulk and weight of the processor are not usually items of concern to the process controller.

The main activities of the mobile robot are planning, perception, navigation and control. The intelligent process controller would also be expected to plan, understand the world and exercise control. Perhaps in the future mobile process controllers would be required, but for the moment, we can ignore navigation.

Robots, as autonomous vehicles, do not have to worry very much about communicating with humans. Some communication might be required, but it is not a current research issue, beyond related work on natural language generation and understanding. On the other hand, process control systems are expected to be intelligible and helpful to humans.

Apart from communicating with humans, this discussion would indicate that compared to intelligent mobile robots, process control should be a piece of cake! So, it is worth looking at how the familiar problems have been tackled.

Data acquisition   Most of the intelligent mobile robots in existence now are research tools and are designed to be flexible, so that sensors can be changed or extra sensors added as required. Many kinds of sensors are used, such as sonar or laser range finders, cameras and communication devices. Interpretation of the data needs to be done as efficiently as possible, which usually means that the more complex sensors have a dedicated computer, running in parallel with the supervisory computer.

Computer architecture   Many mobile robots rely heavily upon visual perception, which imposes a heavy burden of computation. Also, the robot must frequently update its plans in real time, requiring large amounts of processing. Combine this with the sensors and the design and optimisation of the computer configuration becomes a problem. Not only are dedicated microprocessors used for data interpretation, but also for vehicle control and motor control. Communication between processors depends on the requirements of the machine, but might involve serial communication lines or Ethernet. The main processor might be an IBM AT, a Sun or VAX, depending on functional requirements.

Perception and understanding the environment   The robot must be able to make sense of its environment. In many cases, this requires analysing the image from a camera. Computer programs to do this run concurrently with other programs either on the same or different computers. The robot's model of the environment consists of a dynamically maintained data structure. To maintain efficient real-time execution, elements may be removed from the composite model when their presence is not reinforced by sensor readings or the needs of the action level processes. Data from different sensors must be fused, with the associated problems of detecting faulty readings, coping with data of different types and level of perception or just relying on a single sensor for a particular task.

Structure of the knowledge   Straightforward rule-based expert systems are sometimes used for minor tasks, such as obstacle identification. The architecture of the robot means that the expert systems are located on the relevant computer or sensor, so partitioning of the knowledge base is obviously and easily done. Most of the low level perception and navigation tasks are algorithmic in nature, but the higher level decisions, regarding which actions to perform, are based on knowledge relevant to each situation, expressed as partitioned rule sets. In some examples, a rule-based expert system sits at the top of twin hierarchies for perception and navigation, so that the rules trigger procedures for navigation and perception. Much communication between navigation and perception occurs without the expert system being aware, such as procedures for following a wall or avoiding obstacles. Inevitably, top-level control requires the application of poorly organised knowledge.

Planning and decision-making Autonomous mobile robots are programmed with a goal, such as 'Find the control panel and take a reading', and they are expected to devise a plan to achieve that goal. As they move through the environment and events occur within the environment, the plan needs to be updated, including how to cope with obstacles. It is not obvious how much planning can be done in advance, perhaps on the robot's behalf, and what decisions should be left for the robot to make. The robot should also have an appropriate response when its plan fails.

Role of expert systems An expert system is always used to perform high-level decisions and diagnose unexpected events. It may call standard procedures, such as avoiding or removing an obstacle, and wait until another unexpected event generates an interrupt, returning control to the expert system. The data acquisition (sensor) functions and action (effector) functions are handled quite separately, with algorithmic or expert system techniques as required.

The conclusion we could draw from examining research on mobile robots would suggest that processing power should be located on or close to the actual sensors, with the sensors providing some level of data interpretation. Low-level processing at the sensors could be either algorithmic or rule-based. Overall perception, decision-making and planning would be done by an expert system, because of the vague and poorly organised nature of the knowledge. The supervisory expert system is likely to be interrupt-driven, whereas the low-level sensors and effectors would sample at regular intervals. Standard procedures are available for coping with unexpected events, such as obstacles (or faults), executed by the triggering of a rule. Coping with the failure of a plan or failure to understand the world has not been properly addressed. This is an important consideration for process control since it is analogous to the failure of the control system, and would require the effecting of a safe emergency shutdown.

Although rule-based knowledge representations have been widely used, many workers are investigating object-oriented programming.

Mobile, intelligent robots are designed to take much greater control of their interaction with the environment than we would probably expect of a process control system. A robot is expected to understand the world and make decisions with the minimum amount of supervision from a human controller. A process control system could show a similar degree of autonomy, but this is unlikely to be acceptable. There is still a need for human supervision, with the supervisor maintaining his or her own skills, as well as retaining responsibility for the safety and efficiency of the plant. The extent to which process control plants become robot-like is likely to be the subject of debate for some time to come.

6.7 Real-time process control expert systems

As already mentioned, few real-time expert systems have been reported. However, we discuss briefly some that have seen a degree of commercial application. *See* References for further sources of information.

RESCU

RESCU was established under the UK Alvey programme in mid 1984, as a Real-time Expert Systems Club for Users, composed of twenty-one industrial organisations, three universities and one software house. The purpose was to establish the potential of expert systems in process engineering and educate the user community to the managerial and technical issues of expert systems. The chosen application was quality control of an ethoxylates plant at ICI Wilton.

The process is not amenable to conventional, algorithmic process control methods, and requires experienced and highly skilled process operators. Rule-based knowledge representation was used, since at the time that was a well-understood technology. Developments in object-oriented programming since then suggest this would be the preferred paradigm were the project to be repeated now. The knowledge base contains knowledge about plant variables and their relationships with each other. Basic knowledge about the process and engineering knowledge of the plant are also represented. In addition, dynamic facts about the state of the plant are recorded, with carefully managed time-stamping.

The inference processes are based on forward and backward reasoning. Other utilities are available to manipulate the knowledge base, such as a tracker, which monitors the time for each inference activity. A blackboard is used to communicate knowledge between knowledge bases. Uncertainty and the effects of time are also addressed. The ability of RESCU's specifically designed Knowledge Representation Language to represent time in both the left-hand and right-hand side of the rules was considered a major advantage. The possibility of errors in the measuring instruments was included. The RESCU system operates by estimating the quality of the current batch of product, using its knowledge of the process chemistry. When the estimate of quality generates a discrepancy, hypotheses are generated to find the most plausible explanation and the system state updated accordingly.

The RESCU project did not have interface design as one of its priorities, concentrating instead on the feasibility of expert systems for process control. Most of the literature therefore focuses on aspects of knowledge representation and inference.

COGSYS

COGSYS is Son of RESCU, born in mid 1987 and organised as a club of 30 to 40 members, mostly companies in the process control industry, both as users and suppliers of equipment.

The COGSYS system consists of two main parts, the Generator and the Run-Time system. The Generator is a programming environment for the design engineer. The engineer is expected only to be computer-literate and need not be a skilled programmer. The engineer is helped to define the application in a knowledge representation language and fills in forms on the screen to establish the real-time data acquisition interfaces. These allow the engineer to decide whether to keep past values of sensor reading, to maintain a rolling average, look for trends etc.

This information is used to set up the run-time system. Several activities can be performed by this system, such as low-level control, fault detection, alarm monitoring and some diagnosis. The system is programmed by the user, so there is a great deal of flexibility in the tasks that COGSYS can perform.

The more sensors and data manipulation, the greater the burden on the computer, so it is not surprising that COGSYS can be networked. Several computers could be operating under COGSYS and communicating to each other. In this way, some machines could concentrate on low-level control and fault detection, sending signals to a different machine as the need arose for fault diagnosis. COGSYS does not reason about its model of the plant, but can use a combination of rules and classes to diagnose faults and recommend actions.

ESCORT

ESCORT was written by PActel as a demonstration of the techniques of expert systems in the domain of controlling and diagnosing faults on oil rigs. Its justification is often quoted as being to deal with the 'cognitive overload' experienced by operators of process plant. The system analyses the plant data to identify control and instrumentation failures and provides the operator with advice on crisis handling and avoidance. ESCORT uses rules to represent knowledge, with local knowledge about how to control individual control loops as well as deeper, causal knowledge. This allows the system to reason about how one control loop affects another. It has general knowledge about the classes of components that are represented in the plant, as well as knowledge about the specific instances.

In order to cope with the inflow of sensor readings, ESCORT uses two computers. A MicroVAX is used to maintain a database of plant values and to identify the first symptoms of a problem. A special purpose AI machine, a Symbolics, is used to process these 'primary events'. The Symbolics uses its model of the plant and some causal information to figure out what the likely fault is.

ESCORT has some capacity to reason about time. An assertion is tagged with its definition, truth value and links to other assertions. A hypothesis network is established, which grows and contracts as necessary, with the links in the network representing causal connections. When an event occurs, such as an alarm going off, a hypothesis is generated. The system attempts to establish the cause for that event, looking at non-local faults where needed. Prepared test procedures are also stored so that tests for hypotheses can be carried out.

Although ESCORT takes as its justification the need to avoid stress on process operators, the system designers have concentrated their effort on the technical details of the knowledge representation and inference. They report that 'Oil and gas industry personnel . . . have generally been very positive about the usefulness of such a system', but little is available in the literature on appearance, design or style of the user interface.

PICON

PICON was designed specifically for real-time control applications. It was written in Lisp and ran on Lisp machines. Rules were used to represent the domain knowledge, organised into hierarchies. A structured rule editor was available to the knowledge engineers so that correctly formulated rules were easily written using an English-like syntax. The contents of the knowledge base could be displayed using icons, so that users could more easily understand the rules. Other tools were available to classify the rules according to particular system components or states. The user interface was oriented around the use of windows, a mouse, menus and icons. Data acquisition was carried out in parallel, with some facilities for sensor validity checking. PICON could keep up with processes that could be monitored with 'hundreds of measurements per second (though not necessarily the same measurements every second)'.

PICON had a mechanism for focusing attention on areas of the plant where faults were suspected. It could forget out-of-date inferences and log information on sensor values. Operators could interrupt processing to direct PICON's activities. Communication between mulitiple expert systems within PICON meant that many sensors and control activities could have their individual expert systems.

PICON was supplied by LISP Machines Inc and saw several trial applications, but it was expensive to buy and ran on highly specialised and expensive machines. It is still available, but in a modified form.

G2

G2 is available from Gensym Corporation and has been designed for large applications where hundreds or thousands of variables are monitored concurrently. It covers process control, computer integrated manufacturing, monitoring and automatic testing. G2 can run on many familiar machines, from DEC, Sun and Hewlett Packard, as well as on the specialised AI computers from Symbolics and Texas Instruments.

G2 uses objects, dynamic models and heuristics to represent knowledge. The dynamic models may be either heuristic or analytic and can be used to simulate the behaviour of the system before going on-line. Also, they can be used on-line to compare expected with observed behaviour. Historical data are also recorded and can be accessed by the rules and objects.

Emphasis has been placed on the user interface of G2. The screen displays windows and icons and users can tailor the interface to suit themselves. The commands are in 'structured natural language', with a syntax designed for real-time applications. Pop-up menus guide the user so that knowledge may be entered as easily as possible. Explanations of the system's reasoning can be provided, showing which rules were triggered. Trend plots of the values of variables can be displayed too.

G2 uses an 'Intelligent Communications Protocol' so that data processing can be distributed over a network of computers. Data processing tasks, such as scanning and testing, can be delegated to lower-level machines, which then alert G2 as appropriate.

G2 uses forwards and backwards reasoning. When problems occur, G2 focuses on the problem area, using meta-knowledge to guide the focus. Meta-knowledge is knowledge about knowledge, giving advice on how to proceed should particular problem types arise. All data are tagged with a time-stamp as well as a validity interval, so that inferences and calculations may reflect current beliefs about the state of the plant.

MUSE

MUSE is a commercially available AI toolkit, developed by Cambridge Consultants Ltd. It is intended for applications in monitoring and optimisation of industrial processes, the scheduling of manufacturing systems, on-line fault diagnosis, supervisory control and decision support. MUSE applications may be developed on one computer and delivered to run on another, usually smaller, computer.

Knowledge is represented using a variety of languages, although they all share the same set of databases and object structures, so that they can be mixed in the same application. A frame-based system is used, which includes multiple inheritance and demons. The knowledge may be structured in several 'knowledge sources', tailored for each application. A rule-based language is provided for forward chaining and another for backward chaining. Two chaining languages are used in order to employ different pattern-matching and search strategies.

The provision of several knowledge representation and programming languages within the same environment means that facilities can be written in the most suitable language. For example, in a fault diagnosis application, the raw data could be filtered by a program written in C or PopTalk. The filtered data is monitored by a fault detecting module which indicates that an actual or pending fault exists. This would be written in the forward chaining language. Finally, a decision module would monitor the fault hypotheses, displaying information to the operator. This could be written in the backward chaining or frame-based language.

Little mention is made of facilities for communicating with the operator, but MUSE can collect data from sensors and control machinery.

QUIC

The QUIC (Qualitative Industrial Control) project was established in 1986 as part of Esprit in the European Community, with a consortium of seven members. They are developing a toolkit to support the design and development of knowledge-based systems for a wide range of applications in industrial automation. The prototyping applications are on:

- malfunction detection and diagnosis in the thermal cycle of a power plant;
- data interpretation and control of a spacecraft, with assistance for correctance manoeuvres;
- start-up, on-line monitoring and control of the kiln and mill of a cement manufacturing plant.

The toolkit is built around three main languages for knowledge representation. The first is used to construct models of the plant, using libraries of standard components. Different viewpoints of each component are possible, so that a resistor may be considered according to its thermal or electrical properties, for example. Second, a rule-based language is used to express heuristic or empirical knowledge. Third, an event-graph language expresses sequences of possible events. This is used for tasks such as start-up and is similar to Petri nets. An extensive selection of tools are available to support the programmer in the use of these three knowledge representation techniques and to provide various inference mechanisms.

Of the sample systems described herein, QUIC is the most advanced, making use of many of the advances made in techniques and the experience gained from other projects. For example, their approach is firmly embedded in object-oriented programming and they are paying close attention to the validation of the systems. The philosophy underlying the project has been carefully thought out too, so that the disparate projects can be brought together within a sound framework. So far, the project appears to have given little attention to the needs of the eventual users of the knowledge-based systems, concentrating its effort instead on tools to help the designers and builders of such systems. It is hoped that the combination of their well thought out design philosophy and the high quality programming environment that they have chosen will support a good user interface.

LINKman

LINKman, developed by Blue Circle plc and Sira Ltd, is a rule-based expert system toolkit, specifically designed for the process industry. It is described more fully in Chapter 8.

6.8 Where's the user interface?

The previous section indicates that little attention has been paid to the role of the process operator. It seems to be assumed that since the low-level control tasks will be taken over by the computer, then the operator will disappear. It is not difficult to see why this attitude persists and it can be detected in the technical literature on control engineering for the past several years. However, process operators are still with us and the psychologically-oriented literature would assure that they will and ought to remain. The history of automation and employment shows that some skills and job types lose their usefulness, with large numbers of people being thrown into unemployment. However, new skills arise to replace the old, creating new jobs.

While the macroscopic picture would suggest that some kind of work might eventually be found, what of the individual worker who finds that his job is apparently to be taken over by a machine? Elsewhere, we have mentioned that a rule-based expert system is unlikely to represent all the knowledge that an expert has, so the expert system will not be capable of completely replacing the expert. The purpose of installing the machine is to improve the quality and efficiency of production, so it would be better to let the machine take over the mundane parts of the expert's work, allowing the expert to concentrate better on the more difficult and challenging aspects of the job. Hence, introducing an expert system should lead to job redesign, rather than replacement, without the need to de-skill.

When designing the user interface, it is important to remember that there are many ways in which users will want to access the knowledge. The information requirements of the operators will be different from those of the knowledge engineer or the expert, so different versions of the interface might be needed to support the different roles. It is unlikely that a simple expert system could answer every kind of question that the users might ever want to ask, but a certain amount of training can be provided so that the users have realistic ideas of what the system can do. They should know enough about it to trust it enough to use it discriminately and effectively.

A poorly designed interface leads to resistance on using the system. Users complain that the system is 'hard to learn', 'clumsy', 'tiring', 'difficult to use', 'not helpful' etc. A user's opinion of the system is strongly influenced by their experience of the interface – that is what they see, after all. If the interface is unsatisfactory, the users will dislike the system and avoid using it, regardless of all the niceties of the internal program.

When designing the interface, it is wise to avoid creating the impression that the expert system is giving expert opinions in the way that one would expect a doctor, lawyer or other professional to give a considered opinion. Just as one has an option to accept or reject the opinion of a professional, so there have to be limits on the responsibility attributed to the expert system. A user should be aware that an expert system is not infallible. To back up this belief, there should always be the option of calling upon a qualified person to advise on the expert system's conclusions.

In other words, the user interface should not be designed so that the user is made to feel as if humbly kneeling at the feet of an oracle. Instead, the expert system should be like a helpful book that can do some thinking for itself, with the user always retaining the upper hand. The user must trust the system enough to use it and understand it well enough to use it discriminately and effectively.

Chapter 7 Fuzzy rule-based control

7.1 Introduction

In the early seventies, expert systems were being developed in the USA, but in the UK a parallel development was occurring. Rule-based systems, with all the characteristics of expert systems, were being used for laboratory control tasks. These systems used fuzzy set theory to represent the rules and rule-based control has been associated with fuzzy sets ever since. Indeed, rule-based control (rbc) remains one of the most successful applications of fuzzy reasoning.

Although not originally conceived as expert systems, rule-based controllers turned out to have been expert systems all along. So they are also one of the first applications of artificial intelligence to process control. Many applications have been constructed in the intervening years, with some as pure rbc and others as hybrids of rule-based and more traditional techniques. A book on expert systems in process control would be incomplete without a section on fuzzy rule-based control.

This chapter will introduce fuzzy set theory and show how it may be used to present the heuristic knowledge of process operators. An example will be used to explain how control actions are calculated from the rules. Other variations of the original rule-based controller will be described. The chapter concludes with a discussion of the role of fuzzy set theory in rule-based control.

7.2 Knowledge representation

The knowledge representation format for rule-based control is based on the now familiar If . . . Then rule, eg *If the temperature is high and it is not rising quickly, then turn down the oxygen input slowly.*

A rule like this contains several vague terms, which make it difficult to express using conventional techniques. The vague terms are unavoidable, since the rule like this would be taken from the process operator. However, rules of this type may be represented using fuzzy set theory.

Fuzzy set theory was devised by Lotfi Zadeh to cope with exactly this kind of imprecise knowledge. He felt that precision and meaningfulness were mutually incompatible. In the domain of control this is equivalent to forcing the operators to state their control policy so precisely that they no longer believe that it is a statement of what they do.

The difference between fuzzy set theory and normal set theory lies in the degree of membership which elements may possess in a set. In normal set theory, an element is either a member of a set or it is not, ie its membership of the set may take either of the values 0 or 1. In fuzzy set theory, the membership value may take any value in the range 0 to 1. Thus, it is possible to design sets that are based on vague, linguistic terms, such as 'furniture', 'tall men' and 'rich people', the sort of concept that is easily understood in everyday discourse, but is impossible to define precisely. For example, at what height does a person cease being of short or average height and start to be classified as tall? Questions such as this cannot be answered meaningfully with a precise, single value, but fuzzy set theory provides some means of addressing such questions in a useful manner.

In applications of fuzzy set theory, a vocabulary of suitable terms must be defined. We will use height as a simple example (*see* Figure 7.1). The terms are 'tall', 'average' and 'short'. These terms are defined over a suitable range of heights. For men, this would be from about 150 cm to 210 cm. This range is known as the universe of discourse.

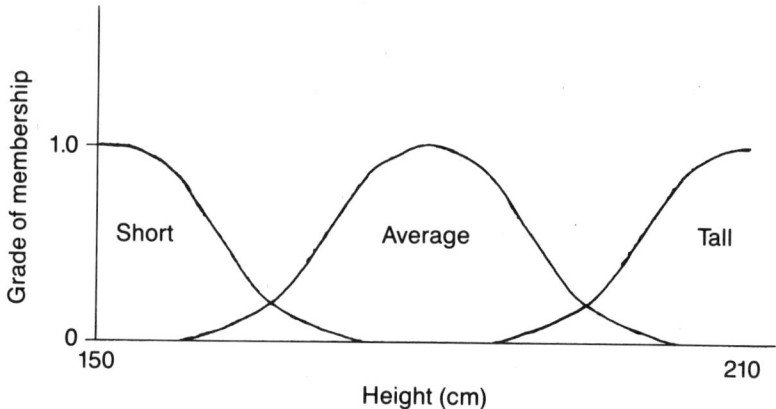

Figure 7.1 Some sample fuzzy sets

For each term, there is a range of values over which it will definitely apply. So, these values would have a grade of membership of 1 in the set defining that term. Similarly, there is another range of values over which that term definitely does not apply, and the values will have a grade of membership on the set of 0. These two ranges do not cover the complete scale, however, and we are left with another 'grey' range where the term has some degree of validity, ie a grade of membership somewhere between 0 and 1.

Normal set theory would assume that the grades of membership are either 0 or 1, with nothing in between. In other words, the scale would be divided crisply in two, with one part representing the heights that are to be understood as 'tall' and the other part representing those heights that are 'not tall'. Fuzzy set theory relaxes this precision, admitting the difficulty of defining precise boundaries.

Note also that the fuzzy sets of Figure 7.1 overlap, so that there are heights which have non-zero grades of membership in more than one set. This is a feature of fuzzy definitions and represents the problems in producing sharply defined, mutually exclusive categories. The lack of mutual exclusivity will be important later in determining the recommended control action.

When representing the rule-based controller, it is advantageous to express it in as general a form as possible, so that it may be easily transferred from one process to another. Rule-based control is similar to PD control, in that the controller output is based on deviation from setpoint and rate of change of deviation, more often called Error and Change in Error. (This is equivalent to PD control and does not imply that rbc can only be used in this manner. Rule-based control has also been used as PID and PI.) Part of the generalisation process is to adopt a vocabulary of terms for Error and Change in Error which is not specific to any domain.

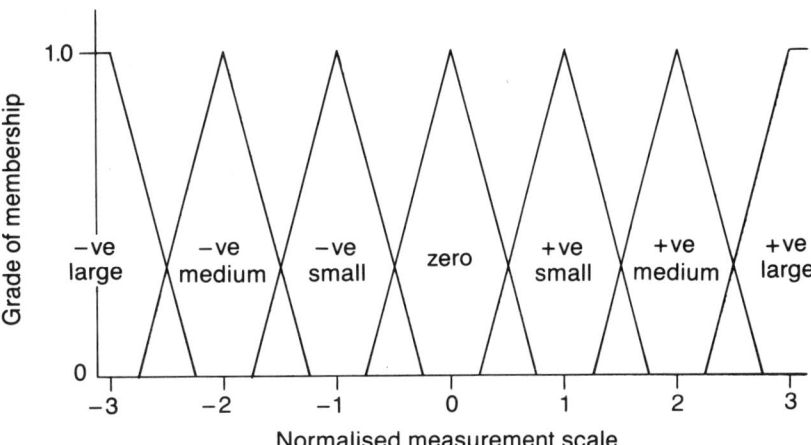

Figure 7.2 Some standardised fuzzy sets

The goal of the controller is to hold the process steady at the setpoint, with no deviation, so Error and Change in Error should both be zero. It is often appropriate to adopt a vocabulary of terms such as that in Figure 7.2 and Table 7.1. The universe of discourse has also been normalised.

To present the rule above, both the temperature and its rate of change are used. Many examples of fuzzy rule-based controllers use a similar combination of a proportional and a differential term, as with PD controllers. A 'space' may be defined which presents

Table 7.1 The fuzzy sets of Figure 7.2 may be represented by the point of the scale on which they are centred

−ve large	−3
−ve medium	−2
−ve small	−1
zero	0
+ve small	1
+ve medium	2
+ve large	3

the proportional and differential terms (*see* Figure 7.3). The scales are often quantised to make programming easier, so that the PD plane consists of a definite number of grid squares.

To cover the PD plane completely would require a rule for every square. The operator may not be able to volunteer quite so many rules and for a complex system, with more than the single variable we are using in this example, a very large number of rules would be required. Also, rules which lie at adjacent positions in the plane will often be very similar. Here, fuzzy set theory can help in an important way.

This is accomplished by exploiting the overlap in the definitions of the terms which lie on the scales. The fuzziness in the definitions means that every fuzzy rule will have a *region of influence*. It will apply with grade of membership unity at some grid square of the plane, and with less than unity in the

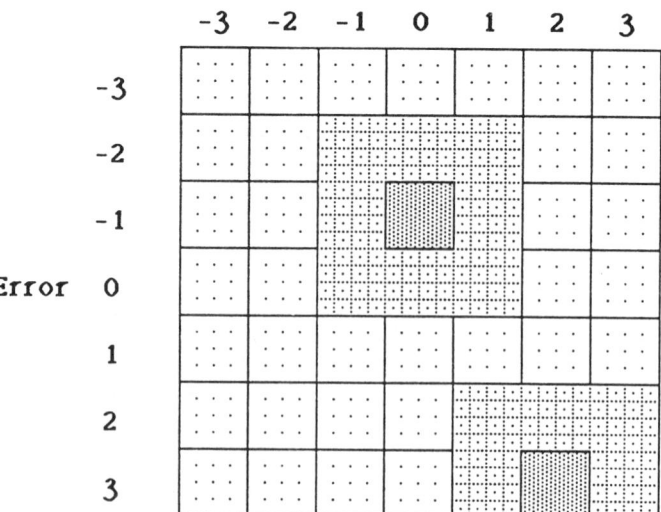

Figure 7.3 A PD plane for the standardised sets

Two sets have been placed on one plane, centred on (3, 2) and (−1, 0). Both sets have an extended region of influence, indicated by the shaded squares.

surrounding region, tailing off until zero grade of membership applies. Since each rule has a region of influence, and the terms on the scale are defined with some overlap, it follows that there will be squares on the plane where more than one rule applies. By taking a suitable combination of the several rules in effect, an appropriate compromise action may be recommended. The total sequence of actions required in the fuzzy rule-based controller is summarised in Figure 7.4.

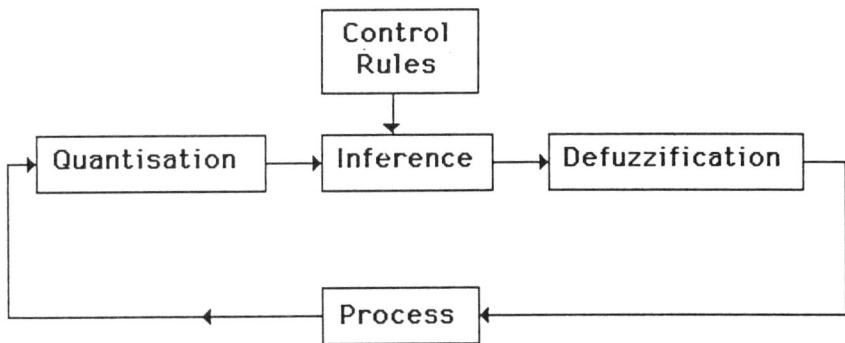

Figure 7.4 Outline of the structure of a fuzzy rule-based controller

In order to represent the rules compactly, each term is identified by the point on the scale on which is centred (*see* Table 7.1). Quantisation tends to produce a lack of fine adjustment in the control action. This may be overcome at the defuzzification step.

The physical representation of the rule, in the case of one observed and one controlled variable, is as a triplet of integers. The first two numbers refer to E and CE for the observed variable and the third is the controlled variable. So, the rule: *If Error is positive big and Change in Error is negative small, then Action is zero.* would be represented by:

{3, −1, 0}.

Each extra observed variable is accommodated by adding another pair of integers to describe its values of E and CE. So the rule: *If Error1 is positive big and Change-in-Error1 is negative small, and Error2 is positive medium and Change-in-Error2 is positive medium, then Action is positive small,* would be represented by:

{3, −1, 2, 2, 1}.

The controlled variables add one more integer to the consequent. Alternatively, the antecedent of the rule may be duplicated, with the appropriate consequent in another rule block. So: *If Error1 is positive big and Change-in-Error is negative small then Action1 is positive small and Action2 is negative small,* could be represented by:

{3, −1, 1, −1}

or

$$\{3, -1, 1\} \text{ and } \{3, -1, -1\}.$$

Many implementations of rule-based control store the rules as an array in the program and not as a distinct rule base. In other words, the rule base and inference mechanism are not stored separately, but this could easily be done. The reason it is not done is for computational efficiency, to meet the requirements of real-time control. Generally, the number of rules required for control is small enough that they may be easily accommodated within the main program.

7.3 Inference mechanisms

As explained in Chapter 4, the inference mechanisms required for rule-based control are much simpler than those required for many expert systems. Refer to Figure 7.4 for a summary of fuzzy rule-based control.

The first stage of the inference process is to map the data onto the quantised scales of the observed variables. This will also require that the readings are multiplied by gains, known as GE and GCE, for the two-term rule-based controller. The settings of these gains is important in determining the response of the controller.

Once the quantised inputs have been obtained, they are compared with each rule in turn. As already explained, the distinctive feature of the rules expressed using fuzzy set theory is that they have a region of influence, given by the spread in the fuzzy sets defining the fuzzy terms. If a particular input coincides exactly with the antecedent of a rule, then that rule is given a degree of fulfilment of 1. However, if the rule falls off-centre but within the region of influence, then the rule has a lesser degree of fulfilment. All the rules are checked to see if they match the input. Fuzzy rules are not mutually exclusive and more than one rule may contribute at a particular control action. These rules do not define an algorithm or decision tree, therefore, but are instead a declarative description of the control policy.

This may be written mathematically as follows:

$$d_i = \min(\mu_{E_i}(e), \mu_{CE_i}(ce))\ i = 1, \ldots, n \tag{7.1}$$

E_i is a term defined on the Error scale, CE_i is a term on the Change in Error scale. E_i and CE_i are the terms of the antecedent to rule i. d_i is the degree of fulfilment calculated for rule i, e and ce are the scaled measurements of the Error and Change in Error scales. The total number of rules is denoted by n.

Measurements of e and ce will produce non-zero degrees of fulfilment only when the appropriate grades of membership in both E_i and CE_i are non-zero.

Once each rule has been inspected, the consequent of the triggered rules (ie those with degree of fulfilment greater than 0) is qualified by that rule's degree of fulfilment. Then, the consequents of all the triggered rules are combined together using the union operation of sets. This produces a recommendation which is the combination of the advice of all the rules.

This may be expressed formally as follows:

$$\mu_{A'}(a) = \max(d_i A_i(a)) \text{ for all } a \epsilon A, i = 1, \dots, n \qquad (7.2)$$

where A' is the fuzzy set representing the recommended action, a is a point on the linguistic scale of action A, and A_i is the consequent of rule i.

The outcome of the inference process so far is a fuzzy set, specifying a fuzzy distribution of control action. However, a single action only may be applied, so a single point needs to be selected from the set. This process of reducing a fuzzy set to a single point is known as *defuzzification*.

There are several possible methods, each one of which has advantages and disadvantages. A method which has been widely adopted is to take the centre of gravity of the whole set. This has the advantage of producing smoothly varying controller output, but it is sometimes criticised as giving insufficient weight to rule consequents which agree and ought to reinforce each other. Other possible methods concentrate on the values of action where the possibility distribution reaches a maximum, called the mean of maxima or average of maxima methods. These methods are criticised as producing less smooth controller outputs.

This may be written formally as

$$a' = \frac{\sum a\mu_A(a)}{\sum \mu_A(a)} \text{ for all } a \epsilon A \qquad (7.3)$$

where a' is the recommended, defuzzified control action. We use summation rather than the integral symbol to indicate that the action scale has also been quantised.

7.4 Example of fuzzy inference for rule-based control

To explain how fuzzy rule-based control works, we will look at a very simple example, using three rules only. Suppose that the rules are as in Table 7.2.

Two vocabularies of terms need to be defined, one for

Table 7.2 Three rules to illustrate how fuzzy rule-based control works
   (1) If temperature High then Medium Decrease to fuel.
   (2) If temperature Normal then No-change to fuel.
   (3) If temperature Low then Medium Increase to fuel.

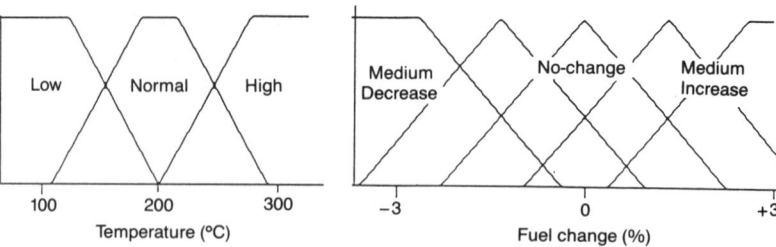

Figure 7.5 Some fuzzy sets for a simple rule-based controller

temperature in the antecedent and one for fuel change in the consequent (*see* Figure 7.5).

Suppose that a temperature reading is taken of 275°. This temperature is checked with the antecedents of all three rules in the rule base (*see* Figure 7.6). For the first rule, this temperature has a grade of membership in the set 'High' of 0.95. This is the degree of fulfilment and is used to qualify the consequent of the rule. So, the set defining 'Medium Decrease' is multiplied by this degree of fulfilment and included in the Action set. The process is repeated for each of the rules, ie the measured temperature is compared with the antecedent set for each rule and the grade of membership is used to modify that rule's consequent. The union of the consequents forms a fuzzy set which recommends the action.

The last stage in the process is to defuzzify the action set. This may be done by a centre of gravity method. In this example, the recommended change in fuel is -2.33 per cent.

7.5 Role of fuzzy set theory in rule-based control

Fuzzy set theory is often associated with the area of rule-based controllers because it was used in the first rule-based controllers that were constructed. However, fuzzy set theory is only a part of the means of construction and not the *sine qua non*.

The persistence of fuzzy set theory in the construction of expert controllers occurs for the same reasons as Mamdani and co-workers were drawn to it in the first place. The main reasons are:

- the knowledge is expressed imprecisely;
- an incomplete set of rules is available;
- process input should vary smoothly.

It has been emphasized throughout that the initial construction of expert controllers relies upon skilled human operators to supply the rules. Assuming that the operators may be relied upon to cooperate, it will still be the case that when expressing their knowledge they will not be able to do so very precisely. Language will remain the means of communication, involving the use of

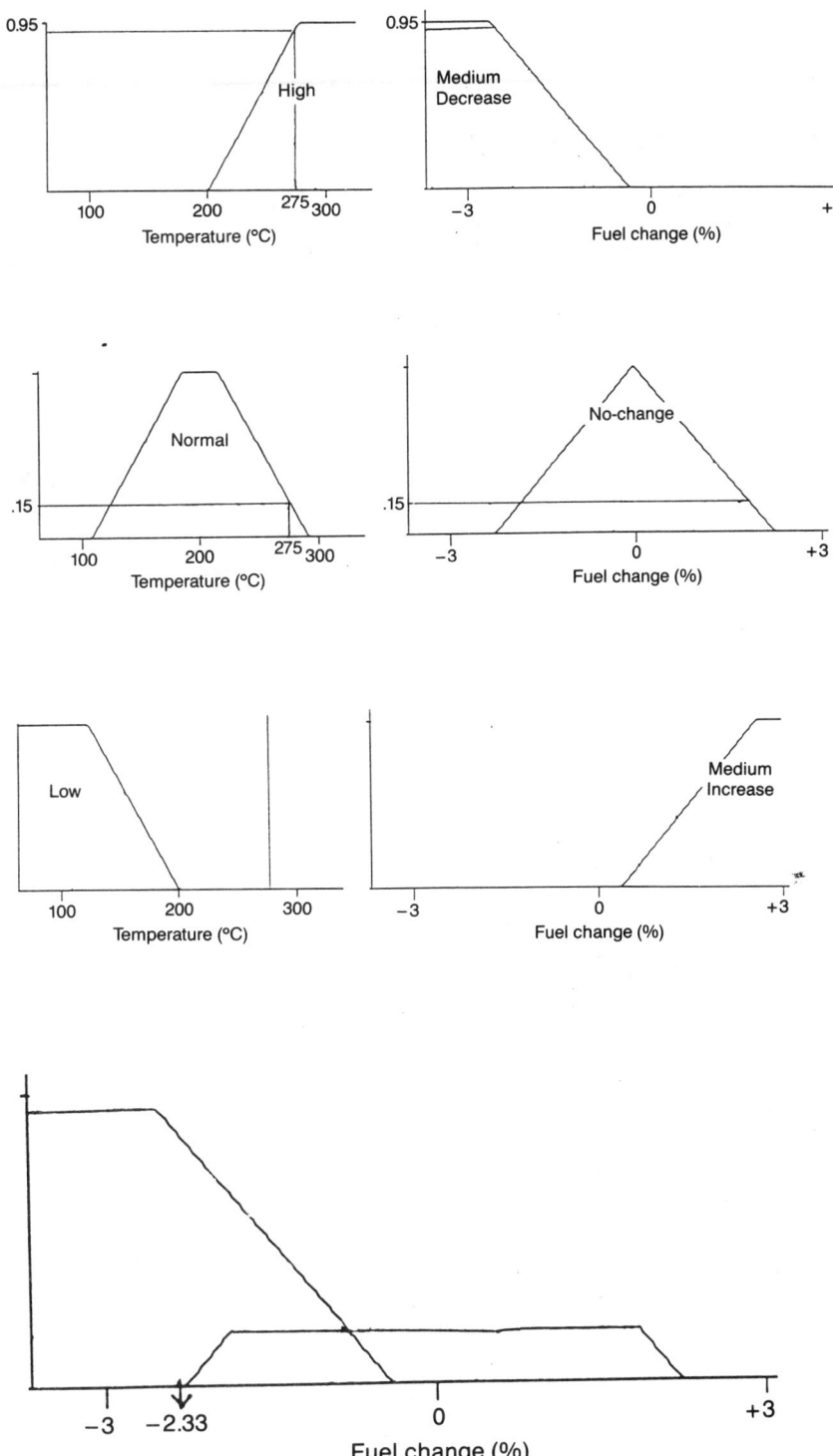

Figure 7.6 The three rules represented by their fuzzy sets

Last stage: defuzzify the action set

terms such as 'slightly', 'high', 'usually' etc, which do not have a precise definition. It is possible to construct devices which oblige the experts to express their knowledge using numerical scales, but this does not avoid the fact that there is unavoidable imprecision in the knowledge itself, because of its nature. Carrying out careful statistical observations of the behaviours of the operators to find the best single action to perform under particular circumstances is a wasted effort if the operators do not know the single best action to perform, but know only roughly what is, in their opinion, the best thing to do.

Hence, we can see that the use of fuzzy set theory eases the three problems outlined earlier. The knowledge that the skilled human operators can provide may not be precise, nor might it be appropriate to represent it precisely. Fuzzy set theory provides a means of representing such knowledge. Where an incomplete set of rules is available, the fuzziness in the definitions of the rules ensures that many regions of the plane will come under the influence of some rule. A catch-all rule may be supplied to cope with the remaining regions where no rule applies. By choosing a suitable combination of rules and their recommended actions, modified by the degree of fulfilment of the rule, the controller will recommend a controller action that varies smoothly across the PD plane.

We should note here that rule-based controllers do not, by definition, require fuzzy set theory. It has been introduced to solve certain problems that arise in the construction of this class of controllers. If fuzzy set theory had not already existed, it would

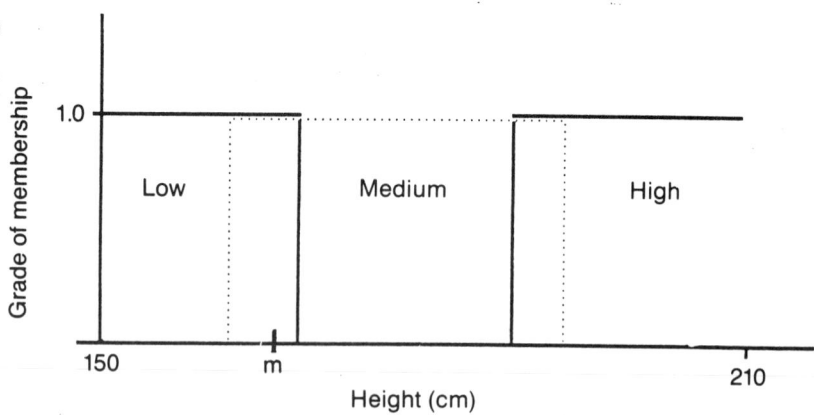

Figure 7.7 Inventing fuzzy sets

If crisply defined sets are used to represent 'Low', 'Medium' and 'High', then the problem of finding a precise boundary between the sets may be partly overcome by arranging the sets to overlap. A measurement which falls in one of the overlapping regions may be weighted according to its distance from the centre of the set's support.

have been necessary to invent something very like it in order to get around these problems.

Consider how this might be done, using crisp sets (*see* Figure 7.7). We have already noted that it is impractical to define precisely the terms that operators use to describe their control actions, there being no point on a scale where 'tall' starts to apply, having not applied before. This may be avoided by using overlapping sets to define the terms 'high', 'medium' and 'low'. Now, when a measurement m is made, as in Figure 7.7, it may well fall inside more than one set. As can be seen, the measurement in the figure falls more to the centre of 'medium' than 'high', so it seems somehow unsatisfactory to give equal credibility to the recommendations of each rule. A possible way around this would be to take the distance from the measurement to the central value of the set. The smaller that distance, ie the closer the measurement falls to the centre, the more credibility we attach to the conclusions from the rules associated with that set. When the measurement falls near to the edge, we associate less credibility. This credibility factor could be used to weight the rule consequents. And *voilà*, we have invented fuzzy sets.

7.6 The self-organising controller

An automatic controller, with control rules derived from the performance of the operators, will have the advantage of consistency, but might not improve very much on their performance. The collection of rules might not be complete or the rules could be flawed in that they could represent a cautions control strategy rather than an optimal or more near optimal strategy. Therefore, it is desirable that the controller should be able to improve its performance above that of the operators, either by amending those rules with which it was initially supplied or by acquiring its own rules. The self-organising controller (SOC) fulfils that purpose. *See* Figure 7.8 for a block diagram of its structure.

Looking again at the state space, we see that the ideal trajectory through the state space is a straight line from the outer corner into the centre. This would represent the process rising directly to the setpoint without overshoot. However, this should be accomplished quickly—there is little advantage in avoiding overshoot if the process is too sluggish.

The self-organising controller is based on the observation that the ideal trajectory lies on the diagonal path throughout the state space. Any deviation of the trajectory from this path should be corrected by modifying the rule or rules that were responsible for the undersirable process behaviour. A buffer is added to record the control actions that were taken in the past. This is implemented by having a *performance table* which is a table the same shape as the state space. Its entries are not rules, but *changes* to the rules. By applying these correction to the consequents of the

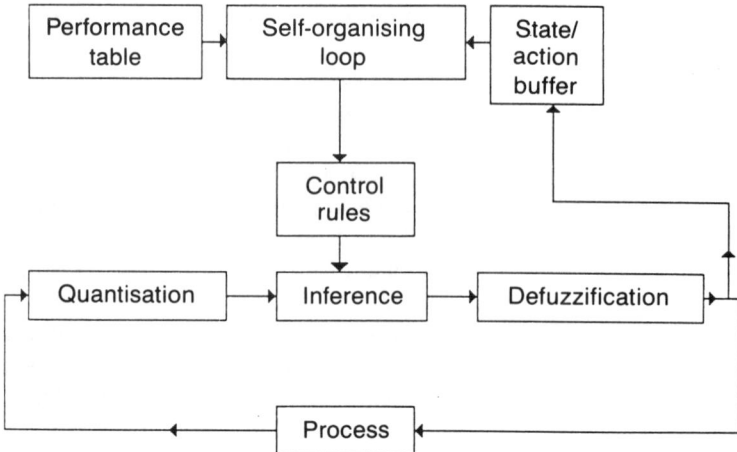

Figure 7.8 The self-organising controller (SOC)

rules, the subsequent passes of the trajectory will be guided back to the desired path.

The performance table consists of a diagonal of zero entries, with entries increasing in absolute value the further away from the diagonal. One half of the entries are positive, the other negative, representing the damping and accelerating effects required of the rules. The entries in the performance table are a measure of the desirability of each possible state in the E, CE space. *See* Figure 7.9 for a sample performance table.

CE

	−12	−11	−10	−9	−8	−7	−6	−5	−4	−3	−2	−1	0
	−11	−10	−9	−8	−7	−6	−5	−4	−3	−2	−1	0	1
	−10	−9	−8	−7	−6	−5	−4	−3	−2	−1	0	1	2
	−9	−8	−7	−6	−5	−4	−3	−2	−1	0	1	2	3
	−8	−7	−6	−5	−4	−3	−2	−1	0	1	2	3	4
	−7	−6	−5	−4	−3	−2	−1	0	1	2	3	4	5
E	−6	−5	−4	−3	−2	−1	0	1	2	3	4	5	6
	−5	−4	−3	−2	−1	0	1	2	3	4	5	6	7
	−4	−3	−2	−1	0	1	2	3	4	5	6	7	8
	−3	−2	−1	0	1	2	3	4	5	6	7	8	9
	−2	−1	0	1	2	3	4	5	6	7	8	9	10
	−1	0	1	2	3	4	5	6	7	8	9	10	11
	0	1	2	3	4	5	6	7	8	9	10	11	12

Figure 7.9 A performance table for SOC

The rules are modified according to the following equation:

$$R(t + mT) = A'(t - mT) + PT(t) \qquad (7.4)$$

where t is a point in time, T is the sampling interval, m is the delay-in-reward parameter, $a'(t - mTF)$ is controller output m sampling intervals ago, $PT(t)$ is the performance table entry calculated from e and ce at time t, and $R(t - mT)$ is the rule that was applied m sampling intervals ago. The consequent of the rule is replaced by the right hand side equation (7.4).

The principal parameter in the design of the self-organising controller is the distribution of correction. This may be done by selecting a single rule which was applied at some fixed interval ago and applying all the correction to that rule. Other schemes have favoured a distribution of correction, reasoning that a single control action cannot be held responsible, but the actions before and after also deserve some of the blame.

Once the decision has been made between whether a single rule or several rules should be corrected, the next decision is how far back in time to go to select the responsible rule. This is the delay-in-reward parameter, m, in the equation above. The original implementations used an interval equal to the dead time of the process. However, it might be possible for the controller to select the value of this parameter itself.

The nature of SOC makes detailed mathematical analysis difficult. It is a heuristic controller, depending for its performance on the characteristics of the process it is attempting to control. Most of the recent insights on the behaviour of SOCs have been obtained through painstaking empirical investigation, but assisted by comparison of SOC with other well-established control paradigms, such as PID or the Model Reference Adaptive Controller. These investigations are shedding light on the interactions between parameters of the controller and leading to better design procedures.

The self-organising controller can help fill in the gaps in the rule-base. It can detect inadequacies in the controller's performance and improve on faulty rules. As a result, a better set of rules should be available.

Self-organising controllers have seen little commercial application, in contrast to rule-based controllers. They are found to be at their best in controlling complex processes, particularly those with dead bands, changing gains or very small or very large gains. Early versions suffered from the quantisation of the state variable, but various methods have been devised to overcome these problems. *See* References for more information.

7.7 'Compiling' the rule base

The controller's rule base should eventually converge on a good set of rules, which the system designer wishes to fix. This could be in order to improve on execution or storage requirements, or simply to prevent any further modification of the rules, either by the self-organising loop of the controller or by manual adjustment. This may be done by 'compiling' the rules down to a straightforward lookup table (*see* Figure 7.10).

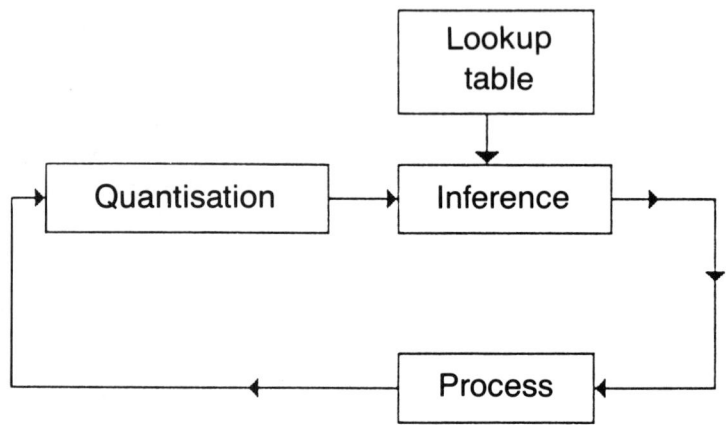

Figure 7.10 The decision table version of the rule-based controller

This table is generated by calculating from the rules the recommended action for every square in the PD plane. If the set of rules is stable, the calculated action at every square will stay the same. These recommendations can then be placed in a table, so that the process input can be obtained simply by looking up a value, based on the process output.

Under these revisions, the controller is very simple and could be programmed in assembly language so as to run very quickly. The disadvantage of the compiled, decision table version of the controller is that it is now no longer possible to distinguish which of the original rules were responsible for recommended actions, so that it would not be possible to identify which needed to be changed. However, it is assumed that the rule set has been deemed satisfactory before the table is constructed.

7.8 Concluding remarks

Rule-based control is becoming accepted now for some kinds of processes, typically those where a mathematical model is unavailable, but human expertise shows that the process may be controlled. Rule-based control can represent the empirically best control strategy, allowing the possibility of consistent control, without the variation caused by shifts of operators. Under these circumstances, a better understanding of the process might be obtained, possibly leading to the implementation of a mathematically-based control method, if the improvement in control so produced would justify the investment. Self-organising control has been studied for some years and its behaviour is becoming better understood, although its still awaits the kind of rigorous demonstrations that industry requires.

It is unlikely that rule-based control will completely supplant mathematical techniques, but there are many applications where such techniques are difficult and unsatisfactory in practice. Rule-based control has a definite role in taming such intractable processes. The next chapter describes one such application.

Chapter 8 Blue Circle case study

8.1 Introduction

The manufacture of cement is one of the most basic industries to any economy. In highly developed, high wage countries, close attention must be paid to material and energy consumption as well as product quality. Blue Circle plc undertook a project in 1982 to introduce expert systems to the control of cement kilns. The project resulted in much higher than expected benefits and also the developments of an expert systems tool for process control which Blue Circle, together with their development partners Sira, are now marketing not only to the cement industry but also to other process industries through Image Automation Ltd.

8.2 Manufacture of cement

Cement is manufactured in three stages: raw material preparation, sintering and grinding. As-dug raw materials, such as limestone and shale, are prepared by being blended and finely ground. During sintering, they are heated to temperatures of about 1400°C in a large rotary kiln. The kilns are typically 4 to 6m in diameter and rotate at about one or two rev/minute. The kilns are lined with refractory bricks and, depending on the manufacturing process have a range of preheating systems. For example the kilns

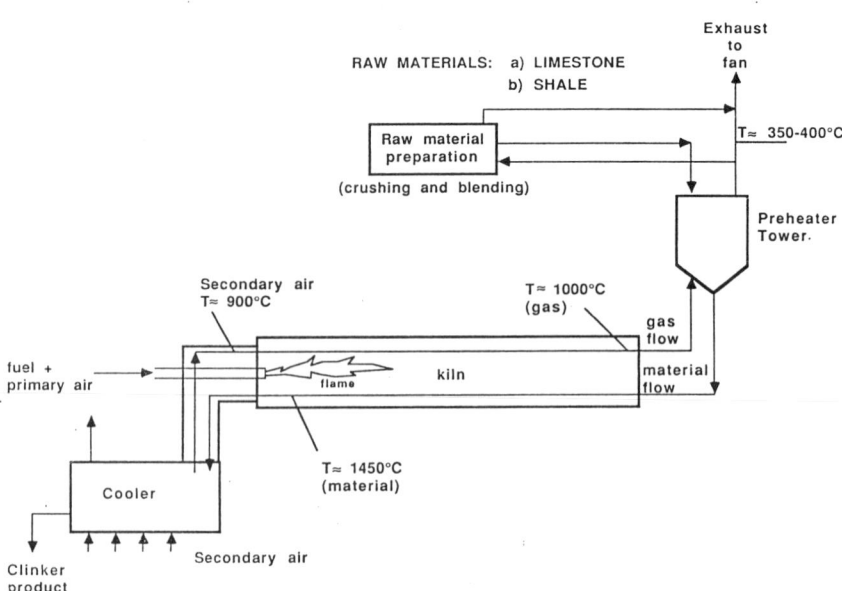

Figure 8.1 Outline of a dry process cement plant

might also contain heavy chains to help the heat transfer from the gases to the feedstock. Figure 8.1 outlines the sintering stage, which consists of:

- feed preheat;
- limestone decarbonation;
- formation of relatively low temperature fluxes;
- reaction of the lime and silica in the presence of the fluxes to form the dicalcium and tricalcium silicates (cement clinker) at very high temperatures;
- the subsequent heat recovery and cooling of the product.

The clinker emerges from the kiln as nuggets, up to about 3 cm in diameter. This material is then cooled, mixed with gypsum and then ground in large ball mills to form cement.

8.3 Control of cement kilns

Although the cement manufacturing process is simple in concept, the control problem is very complex due to:

- the use of natural raw materials of variable chemical composition;
- long process lags;
- large random disturbances;
- the very hostile environment for sensor measurement.

The control of a cement kiln is normally carried out by skilled operators whose key task is to balance the material feed rate to that of the primary energy input in such a way that the resultant clinker is of the desired quality and quantity whilst maintaining steady operating conditions. The operators have to cope with variability in the input raw material and in the fuel. Often, the primary fuel is coal, but, increasingly, low grade fuels and waste products are being used as supplementary fuels, such as high ash coals, used car tyres, petroleum coke, paint wastes etc. These are included because they are difficult to dispose of, except at high temperatures and in the alkaline environment within the kiln. Also, their disposal helps to offset the adverse environment impact of a cement manufacturing plant.

The cement clinkering stages call for temperatures in the order of 1400°C. At these temperatures, typically one third of the feed material is liquid, which causes a coating to form on the surfaces of the refractory bricks that line the kiln. This coating tends to be relatively unstable and therefore the material flow through the later half of the kiln is not particularly steady.

The fundamental control problem is such that multivariable control techniques are required because burning zone temperatures and kiln exit oxygen are mutually dependent variables. For example, a coal change will change both the burning zone temperature and the excess oxygen level. In addition, the responses to fuel and material feed changes are very non-linear.

The operators work under difficult conditions, with few accurate measurements of the conditions within the kiln. The harsh environment causes many sensors to degrade quickly, so that many of the measurements of product quality can only be made by sampling the product and measuring them off-line. Traditionally, experienced operators have been able to make educated guesses at the prevailing conditions within the kiln burning zone by looking at a number of kiln measurements and by observing the process with the naked eye. For example, one of the measurements used by the operator is the torque or power needed to rotate the kiln. When a higher proportion of the material within the kiln is in the liquid phase, so it would stick to the side of the rotating kiln, requiring more power to turn the kiln. So, kiln torque could give the skilled operator an idea of the degree of fluxing and hence of the burning zone temperature. Furthermore, each operator tends to have his own idea of how to interpret the available data and has his own style of carrying out control actions. Since the kiln operates 24 hours a day, the operators work in shifts and, for some cement manufacturing processes, the long process lags of the kiln can be of the same order as the length of the shifts.

The quality of the product is normally measured by the degree of uncombined lime, or percentage free lime, left in the final product. Figure 8.2 shows a typical relationship between this and

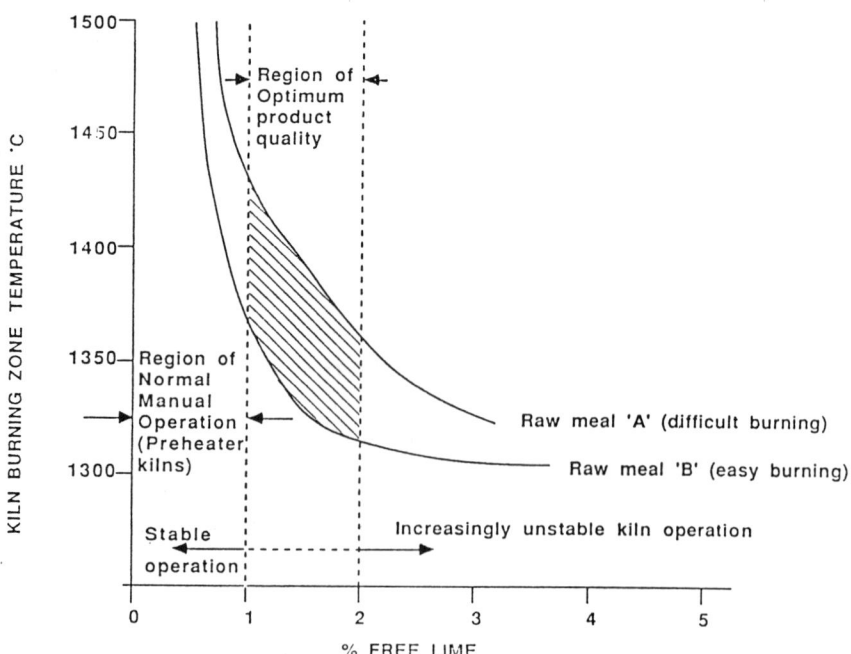

Figure 8.2 Clinker quality as a function of kiln Burning Zone Temperature (BZT)

the peak material temperature in the kiln. Because of the exothermic nature of the sintering process, it is inherently much easier for the operators to err on the hot side than to operate at the less stable but optimum product point because of the increased likelihood of a small reduction in burning zone temperature causing a catastrophic loss of production. Under these latter conditions, all that emerges from the kiln is unsintered feed and dust, instead of clinker.

The industry therefore tends to overburn the clinker, which has several undesirable consequences:

- The final product is degraded, ie less reactive.
- The clinker emerging from the kiln is harder and therefore more energy is required to grind it to a fine powder in the mill.
- The higher temperature in the kiln requires more fuel.
- The refractory lining of the kiln is subject to more wear and tear and needs to be replaced more often. Waiting for the kiln to cool down, replacing the bricks and starting the kiln up again causes loss of production, apart from the expense of the bricks themselves.
- Primary energy input tends to be wasted on volatile cycles within the kiln. In a volatile cycle, salts are vaporised in the Burning Zone, carried by the combustion gases back to the cooler end of the kiln, condense to form deposits and are transported back into the Burning Zone, to be re-vaporised.

The cement industry has attempted to apply modern control techniques, but with little success. Re-examining the work on the application of supervisory kiln control using computers over the past twenty years or so showed that most of the many projects reported were based on mathematical modelling techniques, but that there was little evidence that any of the schemes had been replicated. Conventional mathematical modelling has succeeded best in automating those processes which are well understood and well behaved. However, in a number of more complex applications it has failed to be sufficiently robust to provide a reliably high level of automation. In addition, the mathematical modelling approach has other disadvantages. It is in itself a complex technique, requiring a control engineer to define and maintain the model. Such models are often implemented using programming languages such as Fortran and thus often require staff with computing skills to implement, modify and maintain the model. This makes the understanding of the basis of control poor, which in turn makes the effect operation of such a facility very difficult.

In fact, a 1974 review concluded that *'the future of process control optimisation of fuel consumption and related benefits appears to be dim and that the required development of remote sensors have only been noted in science fiction'*. Mathematical models of clinker production were still lacking in their ability to describe the equilibrium state, let alone the dynamic or disturbed state. Further, many of the important parameters are not capable of being measured directly or reliably. In addition, the non-linear, multivariable nature of the process is difficult to understand. Also, there are large random disturbances and the possibility of long transport lags that can mask the effects of control changes. The whole control problem is extremely complex.

This gloomy conclusion for the future of computer-based control was compared with the relative ease with which human operators could be trained by their peers, and their adequate if sub-optimal control of the plant.

8.4 What to do?

Blue Circle carried out a major review of the clinker making process in 1982. The exercise highlighted the industry's lack of ability to optimise clinker production. The excessively high temperatures at which kilns were being run wasted fuel, so a UK Department of Energy grant was therefore secured to help Blue Circle look into this problem.

The objectives of the project were to achieve a total saving of 30p per tonne of clinker produced (1982 costs). One third of this saving was targetted at direct reductions in primary fuel used, one third from a reduction in cement grinding costs due to the production of softer and more reactive clinker and one third in savings on the refractory lining of the kilns due to lower operating temperatures and better process stability. The total UK cement market was about 14 million tonnes per annum (about 900 million tonnes worldwide), so in total this would be worth £3.6m throughout the UK. If applied successfully worldwide, the savings would approach £350m per annum.

The UK government sponsored project was formalised into five identifiable stages covering:

- Sensors. The identification and development of appropriate on-line indicators of clinker quality.
- Expert systems technology. The identification of microprocessor techniques with the potential to successfully implement supervisory control of the kiln by encapsulating the operators' 'rules of thumb'.
- High level control. To integrate the first two stages into a practical High Level Control system that could optimise plant operation and output.
- Benefits. To evaluate the financial savings associated with the successful application of the technology through a government contracted independent audit.
- Replication. To plan and implement the replication of the technology throughout Blue Circle. Blue Circle have twenty

kilns in the UK alone, so any system devised should be easy to use and demand the minimum of central support.

At that time, the hardware available on the market had made new techniques for sensing and control feasible. Winchester disks, high quality colour VDU's and colour printers were becoming available. The cost of high speed real time computing power had fallen to a point where they were beginning to become a practical proposition for general use within the harsh physical environment of the cement industry.

8.5 Sensors – on-line clinker quality measurement

It was immediately obvious that an improved method of on-line indication of burning zone conditions would have to be found. From this, clinker quality could be inferred.

Various sensors were evaluated, which measured either free lime or NO_x. The free lime monitor was found to be too sensitive to clinker alkali levels on the particular dry process works. The alkali levels were found to fluctuate between −50 per cent and +200 per cent from the daily average of the site. However, under relatively stable and well-defined kiln conditions, NO_x was found to be a very good indicator of peak material temperature in the kiln and therefore of clinker quality. It has proved to be more sensitive than kiln power and has an inherent low signal to noise ratio.

It was expected, therefore, that considerable benefits might arise from being able to operate the kiln so that the NO_x level was at the minimum required to produce optimum clinker quality. At the same time, it would be necessary to ensure efficient combustion through controlling and optimising the concentration of excess oxygen in the kiln exhaust gases. This problem has in the past been virtually impossible using conventional control techniques, because the problem is multivariable. It was the need to solve this complex multivariable control problem that has led to the development of rule-based control as the practical solution.

8.6 Rule-based control

Kiln control seemed to be unsuited to the application of conventional modelling methods, but the human operators displayed considerable skill in controlling the plant, even though their individual styles varied. Therefore, it seemed worthwhile to try to capture the operators' skills in a rule-based expert system for control.

A skilled operator normally expresses his knowledge in the form of rules which describe his control strategy to another operator. The rules are often stated vaguely, with ill-defined terms such as 'high', 'low', 'medium' and 'hot'.

Rule-based control uses a set of rules of thumb which are designed to mimic the thought patterns of an experienced process operator. An example of such a rule might be: *If high (BZT) and high (O₂) then increase feed and reduce fuel.* Where BZT represents kiln 'burning zone temperature' and is normally strongly related to NO_x levels.

As part of the project, Blue Circle investigated a fuzzy controller based on the work of Mamdani and Zadeh. They found it difficult to tune and the original principles of fuzzy set theory were heavily adapted by Blue Circle to meet the real world requirements of process control. The theory behind fuzzy set theory has already been covered in Chapter 7. In short, the technique relies on the use of rules and rule blocks to capture the operators' process knowledge.

The kiln control problem demands a solution that can implement multivariable control techniques. Simple independent control loops would not solve the multivariable problem. However, the characteristics of rule-based techniques are such that multivariable control can be relatively easily implemented. Indeed, Blue Circle did not realise they had a simple multivariable controller until after the event. The resultant knowledge base for a simple two input/two output rule block is shown in Table 8.1.

Table 8.1

If BZT high	*and* Oxygen high	Then Coal 0%	Feed +5%
If BZT high	*and* Oxygen OK	Then Coal −2.5%	Feed +2.5%
If BZT high	*and* Oxygen low	Then Coal −5%	Feed 0%
If BZT OK	*and* Oxygen high	Then Coal +2%	Feed +2%
If BZT OK	*and* Oxygen OK	Then Coal 0%	Feed 0%
If BZT OK	*and* Oxygen low	Then Coal 0%	Feed −2%
If BZT low	*and* Oxygen high	Then Coal +5%	Feed 0%
If BZT low	*and* Oxygen OK	Then Coal +2.5%	Feed −2.5%
If BZT low	*and* Oxygen low	Then Coal 0%	Feed −5%

If the kiln and oxygen readings deviate from their respective setpoints then these rules could be used to calculate kiln fuel and material feed changes. These changes are downloaded to the plant at regular intervals of around twelve minutes. The external setpoints of the kiln coal and feed controllers are adjusted in line with the rule block outputs.

In the case of the wet process for cement manufacture, the use of three input/three output rule blocks were found to be necessary in order to achieve good control. Rule-based control techniques can easily be extended to cover many variables, but it is interesting to note that Blue Circle found that most operators only conceive of a two-input control problem at any one time. The particular pair of inputs in likely to vary considerably, however.

The above rules are very important in the optimisation of kiln burning conditions, but alone they do not cover all the instabilities inherent in kiln operation. Other rule blocks need to be constructed and combined to form a 'Control Strategy' which identifies non-standard kiln conditions, such as the onset of CO due to a major kiln disturbance (ie carbon monoxide in high concentrations), and make appropriate changes to the plant in order to regain kiln stability. So, when the kiln was subjected to a major disturbance, such as the result of a kiln preheater cleaning or coating breaking off, a dedicated rule block or specific strategy to counter the particular disturbance could be quickly developed and incorporated in the Control Strategy. In practice, the majority of on line control time is spent in handling normal conditions or minor disturbances by making small but relatively frequent

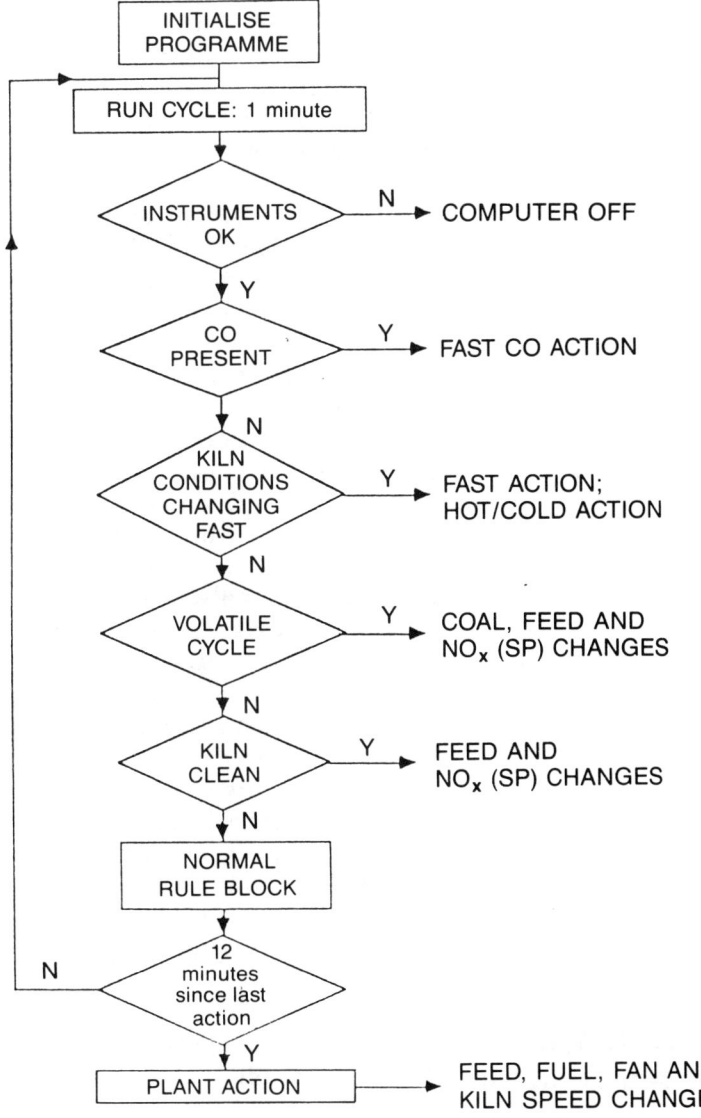

Figure 8.3 Outline of the rule-based control program

changes, ie four or five times an hour, to the plant control parameters. An outline structure of the complete program is in Figure 8.3.

8.7 Practical experience

By 1982, F.L. Smidth in Denmark had launched a fuzzy controller for cement kiln control and Blue Circle were able to evaluate it on a large 0.6 million tonnes/year dry process kiln at the Hope Works in Derbyshire. It was well known that the particular kiln was difficult to control and the exercise showed that the fuzzy controller when combined with the use of NO_x measurement, could adequately supervise the plant. It was, however, unable to meet the energy optimising criteria. The project had now reached the point where the problem was how best to capture and represent on computers the operators' process knowledge. Blue Circle decided to design their own customised solution and subsequently commissioned Sira to collaborate on the project. The problem became how best to capture the process knowledge and subsequently use it to develop a robust, computer-based, supervisory kiln control system.

The development of the resultant 'linguistic' control system was carried out on the same works as before. The controller software was specifically designed to be very much more deterministic and a great deal of effort went to ensure that it was as fail safe as possible. This new approach proved to be very robust with respect to handling process disturbances and capable of controlling the kiln at much lower temperatures than had previously been considered practical. It was fine tuned within four months and the strategy was subsequently transferred to a second similar kiln on the same site within a few weeks. The same strategy has subsequently been transferred to another site at Aberthaw in South Wales and was again on-line within a matter of hours and fine tuned within a few weeks. Subsequent experience indicates that the High Level Control development time for a new cement kiln process control strategy, once the team is familiar with the technology, takes about six to eight weeks and subsequently only three to four weeks to transfer to a second site.

Blue Circle are committed to replicating the technology on all their works throughout the UK, and in July 1988 some 4.5 million tonnes of cement making capacity were under High Level Control, equivalent to one-third of the total UK cement-making capacity. The LINKman expert system was developed to enable the replication of the technology.

8.8 Knowledge acquisition

The task of knowledge acquisition was simplified to some extent by the availability of a published kiln operation rule set. This rule set was however by no means complete and the control philosophy was not directly applicable to the Hope kilns. Nevertheless, all the initial knowledge acquisition was conducted by research personnel from Blue Circle who had no previous knowledge elicitation experience but who did understand both the process chemistry (deep knowledge) and the operation of the kiln. Knowledge engineering, ie both the process of structuring the knowledge and implementation in the machine, were again conducted by the same research staff. Although they had previously had some limited experience of computer systems, they would not have described themselves as knowledge engineers or software specialists.

8.9 Impact on personnel

One of the very practical aspects of applying this type of technology is the effect on the workforce and management. During the early development phases of the project, these aspects were extremely critical. As time progressed, lessons were learned and greater confidence gained. These aspects are no less important, but are fortunately less critical.

A typical project covers seven stages and these are reviewed below.

Initial project formulation and site visit

The initial reaction of the workforce is essentially one of concern over job security and to a lesser extent over job satisfaction. It was therefore most important that the project was explained to the workforce as an aid to the operator in the form of an autopilot and that he would remain in charge of the plant at all times. It is also useful to stress that it improves job security through improved product quality and reduced costs.

It is important to identify the right person to become project leader or project engineer within the works with the correct blend of technical skills and management responsibility at this time. Senior management must also be seen to be strongly committed to the project in the early stages.

On-site knowledge elicitation

During this phase, the operators are heavily involved since they are the source of the basic rule-based knowledge and in particular because they know the idiosyncrasies of the plant under consideration. Their knowledge then needs to be combined with practical technical understanding of the process and then encapsulated by the project engineer into the overall high level control strategy.

Initial training

The works project leader and his deputy require approximately three to five days of off-site hands-on training. Since Blue Circle's system had been designed to be user friendly, no particular problems occurred at this stage for either computer literate or computer illiterate personnel.

The on-site training covers both the control room personnel and management in general. The management training covers the overview of the project and its likely effect on the site while the operator training concentrates on the use of the operator interface and system menus. At this stage, the operators tend to be sceptical of the power of the system. Some are positively helpful while others less so. Generally speaking, it is fortunate that the more helpful tend to be the better operators. Management, however, have proved to be not particularly good at attending the briefing sessions.

Initial commissioning of the system

Since this normally involves those who have attended the off-site training course, there is little problem at this stage. Most of the work is carried out in the background and involves connecting wires and configuring the system database.

High level control strategy development

This phase is high risk. Careful handling of the project is vital at this stage because it is important that strategy development is rapid in order that any undesirable process disturbances are minimised and goodwill generally maintained. This generally calls for twenty-four hour cover during the early stages of commissioning in order to gain the goodwill of the shift personnel. The commissioning engineer must be strongly committed to the project in order to be willing to babysit the initial control strategy through this most testing phase. The project engineer at F.L. Smidth, J.J. Østergaard, has been known to sit with his controller for 50 hours without a break. Even now, eighteen to twenty hour stretches during the critical first two or three days are not unknown. The early stages of commissioning can provide a very valuable training exercise for the engineers from the host site. Unfortunately, they are too often disinclined to participate fully.

The methodology behind strategy development is one of trying out the simplest control strategies possible based on a combination of the pragmatic knowledge of the operators and technical understanding of the process. The development must be incremental and fast so that strategies can be built and evaluated within one cycle time on the process or one per day. At this stage, before widespread experience had been gained of the new technology, management could seriously restrict strategy development because of lack of understanding of the characteristics of applying rule-based control. The technology thrives on rapid prototyping and evaluation of control concepts. For example, it is important that more than one variable can be manipulated and tuned at the same time.

In the case of operators, there is initially very little problem in getting the system on-line since the proposed changes are normally similar to the control actions they would make, but very much smaller and more frequent. Once on-line, an adequate strategy should be operating within the first few days.

Operators at this point generally begin to be concerned about their job security unless management is positive in allaying their fears. The initial honeymoon atmosphere can evaporate for a number of reasons and the operators move on to a relatively uncooperative phase by insisting on operating the plant manually for long periods. Since they are always responsible for the plant, this is difficult to counter. The project team then has the problem of getting back into a strategy development mode and the speed with which this can be achieved is strongly related to management's committment to the project.

Another hurdle that can arise at this stage is where, once strategy development has been initiated, some critical plant item is found to respond inadequately. Under certain circumstances, commissioning has to be delayed for several weeks until the item is put right. Alternatively, the quality of control is seriously degraded by the item in question and therefore strategy evaluation is more difficult and overall progress hindered.

Post commissioning support

The post commission support phase has proved more important than originally envisaged. Although an effective high level control strategy for a cement kiln can be developed and tuned within two to four weeks, there is a major problem in transferring the knowledge contained within the strategy to the plant personnel and in developing their skills to tune the system. This is important since the relatively short commissioning time means that the control strategy is probably incomplete in that not all types of perturbations will have been seen and the corresponding strategy developed. This period of observation could span many months under some circumstances.

In addition, there is a strong tendency either to blame the system and switch off or try to modify the strategy the first time the plant performance is below expectation. The former should not occur since if the system does not perform well, there is generally a good process reason for it. The source of the problem needs to be identified and corrected as quickly as possible before the rather fragile operator goodwill is lost.

In the second case, there is a possibility that the site personnel can accidentally de-tune the strategy to the point where it no longer controls well. There is therefore a real need for a low key post commissioning 'hand-holding' phase to ensure that the strategy is adequately developed as well as ensuring that the site people are fully conversant with the system.

Identification of benefits phase

The benefits, in the case of a cement process, are generally fairly difficult to quantify because the performance of these types of plant are by their nature not very consistent. In particular, the base line is constantly changing due to raw material changes and process plant modifications and management is therefore reluctant to allocate benefits to any one project. The key to successful implementation is for management to be committed to the technology and so ensure high percentage of on-line times. If this is not forthcoming, then uncertainty leads to poor running times and greatly reduced benefits. It is ideal if management can qualitatively recognise the wide range of benefits arising from applying expert system technology without having a major allocation of resources to prove the benefits.

8.10 LINKman

In order to tackle the problem of the high cost of replication, Blue Circle contracted Sira (the UK high technology contract research organisation) to produce an appropriate customised system in the absence of any practical commercially available host system. This development resulted in LINKman.

The hardware configuration (Figure 8.4) was chosen to be capable of being easily supported around the world. The system is based on the DEC 11/73, is written in C and assembly language and runs under the RSX-11M operating system, and soon RSX-11M plus. This permits full multi-user and multi-tasking facilities, allowing simultaneous use by engineers and operators through the use of menus. A microvax version is now available. A wide range of control room specific management information and reports have been built in and it has been specifically designed to not only control up to eight independent pieces of plant, but also to sit either beside any of the present generation of centralised display systems or on its own. One unit has already proved capable of controlling at least three kilns simultaneously. The control of at least three kilns or an equivalent combination of kilns and mills probably represents the likely upper limit of the present system.

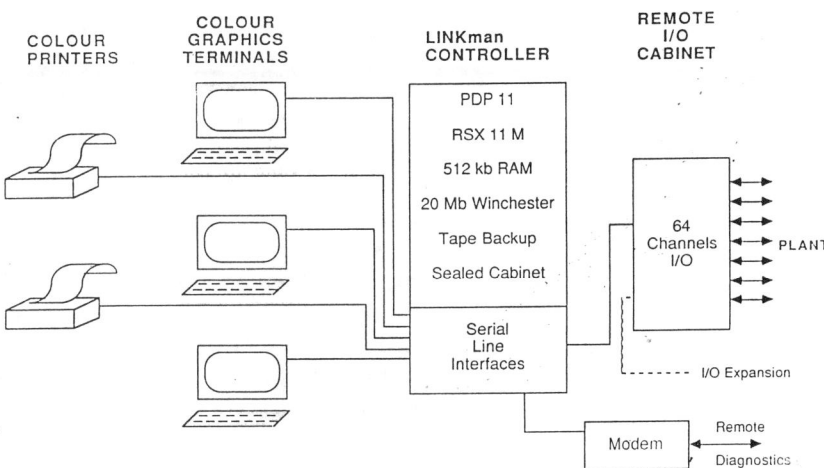

COLOUR PRINTERS

COLOUR GRAPHICS TERMINALS

LINKman CONTROLLER

REMOTE I/O CABINET

PDP 11

RSX 11 M

512 kb RAM

20 Mb Winchester

Tape Backup

Sealed Cabinet

Serial Line Interfaces

64 Channels I/O

PLANT

I/O Expansion

Modem

Remote Diagnostics

Figure 8.4 Typical configuration of LINKman for a cement works

The main characteristics of the LINKman system are listed in Table 8.2. It has been designed to mimic the actions of the operator and at any point when strategy development is not going well, it is prudent to go back to first principles and remember that the system should be mimicking both the thinking and actions of the operator. This return to first principles normally helps find a solution to the problem.

Table 8.2 Main Characteristics of LINKman*

1 The use of linguistic rules to capture the process knowledge
2 The controller is a form of variable gain, multivariable set point controller.
3 The controller has the ability to:
  (i) switch between different rule blocks;
  (ii) self check the integrity of the system;
  (iii) implement Boolean logic;
  (iv) accept operator and laboratory data;
  (v) hand back to the operator when conditions are uncertain, ie may be used in a similar manner to that of an autopilot.
4 Strategy development is simple, incremental and fast.
5 The strategy is very visible and is based on mimicking the action of the operators.
6 It can present plant or control logic information to the operator in an easily readable and useful way.
7 It offers management process information and logging facilities.
8 It is typically more consistent than the human operator.
9 Control strategies for specific process have been found to be very portable.
and most important of all
10 It has the power to implement high level control strategies, ie product and process optimising control strategies.

* This table was prepared by members of Blue Circle plc

Although the heart of the system is the rule-based control element, it is nevertheless only one part of the system. Data acquisition, logging, trend analysis and management reporting functions are all included together with a comprehensive engineering toolkit. Attention has also been paid to the user interface (which in this system is totally menu-driven) in an attempt to maximise the ease of use.

At the system design level, considerable attention has been paid to the nature of the knowledge, the functional requirements and the methods of use of the system. The conceptual design is shown in Figure 8.5 and conforms with the normal architecture associated with expert systems. In keeping with this, all the elements have been functionally separated, to keep the knowledge explicit and separate from the inference and control mechanisms.

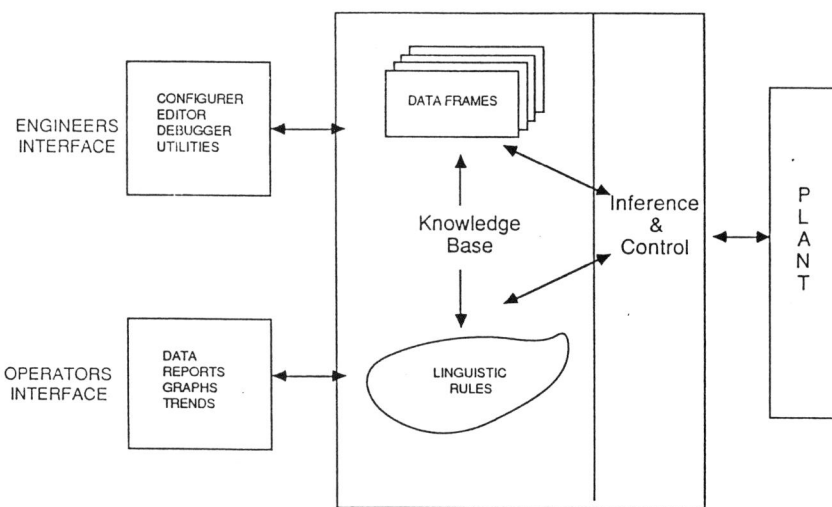

Figure 8.5 LINKman architecture

In the process world, the knowledge takes two main forms. Firstly, there is a knowledge about the plant instrumentation, ie the devices such as pressure and temperature sensors. Knowledge about these sensors includes their physical and electrical properties, together with the plant specific knowledge such as their naming and address assignments. Associated with this is knowledge about the nature of the measurement, expected normal values, alarm limits, engineering units, smoothing etc. There may also be fixed algorithmic operations which are required: calculation of rates of change, regression and cross correlation are typical examples. Secondly, there is knowledge of the plant, the process and its operators. This is usually a mixture of prescribed procedures, heuristic rules and deeper process knowledge.

Two types of user interface were designed, one for use by the engineer and the other by the process operator. The engineer's role is to define the plant items, prescribe the process measurements and to establish the control rules and procedures. In addition, the engineer, who is in consultation with the plant operators, builds the screen displays and graphics by which the operators are kept informed about the operation and status of the process. The operator functions are designed to give the users access to the process information and are primarily display related.

Many expert systems are aimed at making the expert's knowledge available to the non-expert and explanation of the advice given in such systems is important, not only because it can give confidence to the user, but also because of its teaching role. In process control, the targetted users are the operators, most of whom have an excellent knowledge of process operation, although they may lack deep knowledge. In this situation, the operator requires a clear and regularly updated display informing him of the control action advised or implemented. The operator is therefore provided with a display showing the rules which are currently being applied and their degree of fulfillment. The question 'Why?' is rarely relevant in this particular context.

It is interesting to note that many other industries that rely on human operators to control their plant have expressed an interest in the approach since it is proving to be a very powerful general purpose control tool. In fact, one system was evaluated under the auspices of the Sira Industrial Expert Systems Club Project where the test bed was a BP lubricating oil plant. (BP have since bought LINKman and experienced a payback period of 12 months.) The system is a general purpose toolkit and as such could be configured for use by any industry. It is likely that the technique can be applied to any process that is presently dependent upon an operator taking note of analogue signals and other process data and subsequently making set point changes to his process. For example, Blue Circle intend to apply LINKman to cement mills, once an on-line particle analyser becomes available. It is possible that the controller could be applied to cover the cooler, raw milling and other on-site processes whose performance could be improved. Although the initial application has been in the manufacturing of cement, and whilst some of the detailed design has been driven by the requirements of the cement industry, the overall approach adopted makes this system suitable for application in a number of quite different processes.

8.11 Benefits

The application of High Level Control using LINKman has proved to be more successful than originally anticipated. Not only have standard fuel consumptions been reduced by up to 10 per cent but

NO$_x$ levels have been significantly reduced. In addition, general working practices have been improved and the thermal stress on the refractories has been greatly reduced. These all arise from being able to control the kiln nearer to the optimum operating condition as indicated in Figure 8.2.

Independently audited overall savings in excess of 94p/clinker tonne have been seen at the Hope Works. A reduction of 7 per cent in kiln fuel consumption was achieved, equivalent to a cost saving of 50p per clinker tonne. This was enhanced by a further saving of 44p per tonne on electricity costs, due to the reduction in grinding power resulting from the production of a softer, more reactive clinker. It was not possible to identify further savings in refractory lining costs during the period because of the relatively short monitoring period, but consistent operation at lower burning zone temperatures is confidently expected to result in significant long-term refractory savings. This is a saving *three* times greater than that originally expected. And many other secondary benefits have accrued too.

In practice, the control problem had to be tackled on two levels, first to control the plant and handle normal process perturbations efficiently which is reflected in reduced standard deviations of key parameters, and second to optimise the plant with respect to product quality, energy and raw material usage.

In terms of energy savings, the targetted savings have been achieved and exceeded. On the 1.2 million tonnes produced annually at Hope, this would mean a minimum annual saving of £930,000 making a typical payback time of less than 3 months. In

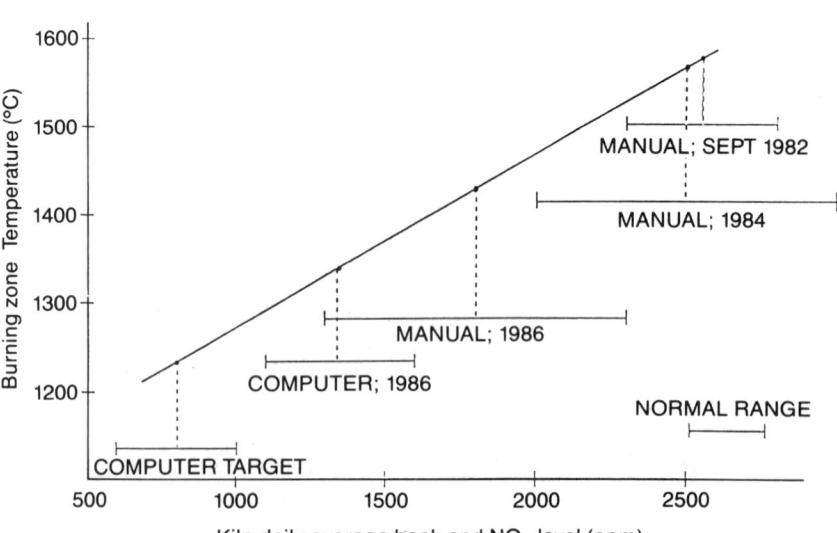

Figure 8.6 Improvement in NO$_x$ emission level as Burning Zone Temperature declines

addition to the financial benefits, the other benefits which are normally associated with an expert system approach to problem solving have been realised.

More specifically, in terms of NO_x and kiln temperatures, the average NO_x levels have been reduced by up to 50 per cent from earlier NO_x monitoring periods and this has been reflected in a 100 °C to 200 °C drop in average burning zone temperature and at least 100 °C drop in peak burning zone temperatures (*see* Figure 8.6). The improvement in NO_x emissions earned Blue Circle and Sira a Better Environment Award for 1987. High Level Control, in reducing the daily average burning zone temperatures, typically generates a 10 per cent increase in output, together with a 5 per cent to 10 per cent reduction in standard fuel consumption.

The difference in kiln performance between manual and computer control is shown in Figures 8.7 and 8.8 from a third works. In the case of computer control, the standard deviation of the key control parameters can be seen to be greatly reduced. The lack of major plant perturbations is also very noticeable.

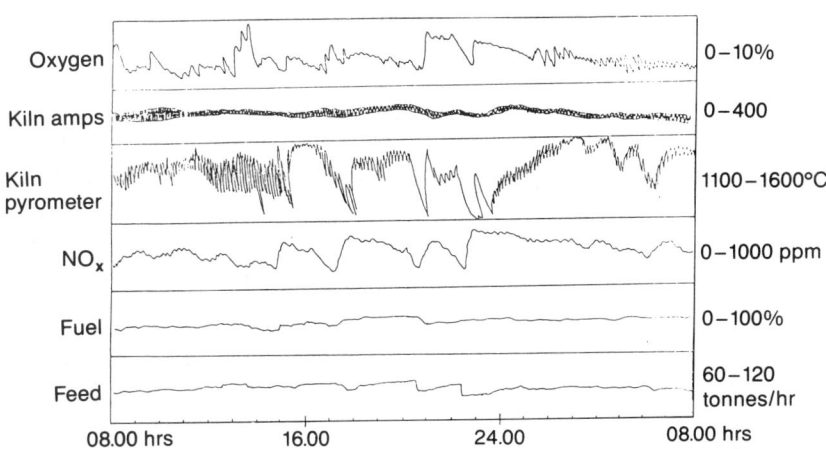

Figure 8.7 Manual control of a kiln, January 1986

The change in grindability under hard and soft burning conditions resulted in a 15 per cent reduction in the grinding energy to produce clinker to the same surface area. When the increased reactivity of the soft burnt clinker is added to this, the overall reduction in mill power on this works in order to achieve the same 28 day strength is in the order of 30 per cent.

Another interesting observation is that it initially takes at least two weeks (on preheater kilns) for the kiln fuel savings and increased outputs to fully develop. This is thought to be associated with the kiln lining rebuilding itself and the volatile cycles settling

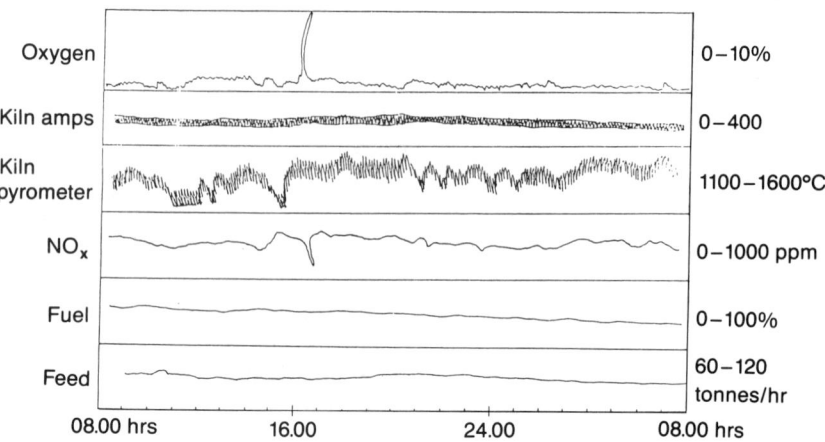

Oxygen		0–10%
Kiln amps		0–400
Kiln pyrometer		1100–1600°C
NOₓ		0–1000 ppm
Fuel		0–100%
Feed		60–120 tonnes/hr

08.00 hrs   16.00   24.00   08.00 hrs

Figure 8.8 Computer control of same kiln; April 1986

down to much reduced levels. There is also a strong indication that there is a substantial lag of several days in the NO_x/fuel relationship. Again, this is probably due to the time required for the interaction between the unstable control and volatile cycles to reach a new equilibrium.

Blue Circle have applied LINKman to wet, semi-wet and dry process kilns. Experience to date has shown that the apparently simple and amenable wet kiln process requires the more complex control strategy. This is due to the need to take account of the very long natural cycle time of the process, 10 to 14 hours, well in excess of one shift, and the difficulty of achieving both stable and optimum operating conditions when under manual control. The improved stability of the kiln can also be seen in many ways including the more stable volatiles content of the clinker. By being asked to develop the technique for the more difficult kilns of the Group, Blue Circle and Sira have developed a more powerful control strategy which in turn has resulted in much greater than anticipated benefits.

The system has also been shown to be capable of quickly and efficiently stabilising a kiln that has not been brought up to feed very smoothly under manual control after a short stop. This can be seen in Figure 8.9 which is a trend log of a semi-wet process kiln during the starting phase. On this kiln, the natural cycle of the kiln has been found to be about three times (12 hours) the mean material throughput time of 4 hours. Similar cycles have been seen on both wet and dry kilns. It is the complex nature of these very long cycles that enables LINKman through the application of consistent high level control strategies to control the plant better than the group of shift operators and so achieve the higher than anticipated savings.

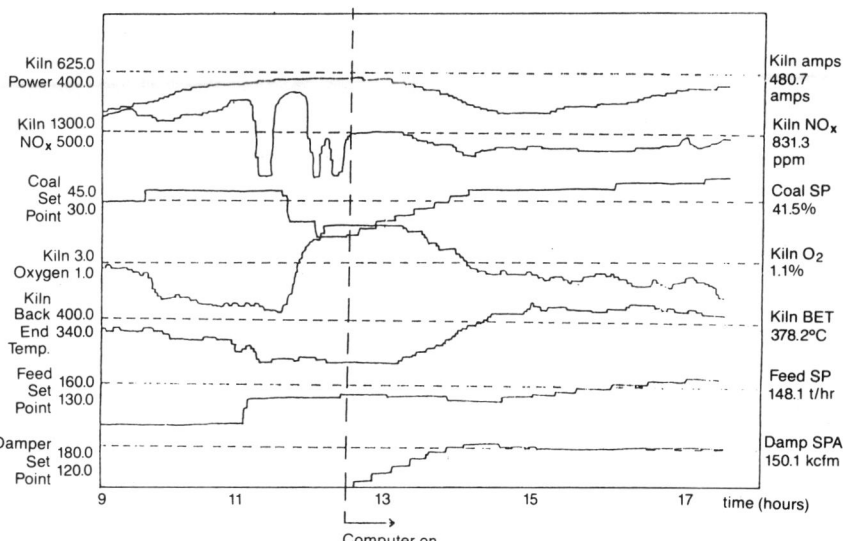

Figure 8.9 Transfer from manual to computer control of a semi-wet works kiln, October 1986

The knowledge is explicit and the heuristics and control actions represented linguistically. This has resulted in a greater level of visibility and understanding and this has resulted in the fact that the system is used with enthusiasm and little difficulty by the operators. There have also been some unexpected benefits, perhaps the main one being that the facilities provided permit rapid prototyping. This has greatly helped in the exploration of new ideas and as a result Blue Circle have gained a deeper understanding of parts of the process.

Indeed, the improvement in Blue Circle's understanding of the cement manufacturing process has been much greater than expected. For example, the extent to which energy was wasted in maintaining volatile cycles had not been realised before.

8.12 Summary

Over the last five years Blue Circle and Sira developed a rule-based controller that is now in the process of being replicated throughout the Group. In the absence of an adequate commercially available system, the new system had to be custom designed, and this has resulted in the launching of the LINKman system.

The controller has proved to be very robust and the control strategies developed on it using the LINKman toolkit are also very easily transferred from site to site. Strategies for new processes have also been shown to be capable of being developed very quickly and are easily maintained. Operator training is also simple and quick.

The benefits arising from the control strategies developed by Blue Circle are proving to be very substantial in that fuel savings of up to 10 per cent are being found, together with many other serendipituous benefits. These appear to be well in excess of 100 per cent greater than those reported elsewhere. This has been attributed to the fact that LINKman is a second generation rule-based controller, specifically designed for process control application and had the added benefit of being developed on very difficult plants. It is also that a very significant proportion of the overall benefits are associated directly with the achievement of tighter supervisory control alone.

Table 8.3 Benefits arising from High Level Control of the cement process*

1 Standard fuel consumption is reduced substantially.
2 Clinker outputs can be increased over and above that which is in line with the reduced standard fuel consumption.
3 Product quality and clinker grindability are significantly improved.
4 Milling costs are reduced in line with the improved product quality and grindability.
5 Key process parameters are controlled more closely, eg NO_x, O_2 fuel and free lime.
6 Kiln exit NO_x levels are significantly reduced.
7 The knock-on effects of process disturbances are minimised.
8 Refractory peak temperatures and cyclic thermal stresses are reduced.
9 Refractory life is increased.
10 Kiln running times are improved.
11 Kiln-specific knowledge concerning the process and process dynamics is greatly enhanced.
12 Improved working practices can be developed.
13 High Level Control superimposes a consistent approach to control and eliminates the normal shift variations.
14 The routine workload of operators is reduced.
15 There is a powerful data collection and logging facility for use by management.
16 Improved control provides the oportunity for management to better manage the process and its operation.

* This table is based on information provided by members of Blue Circle plc

In terms of cement kiln control, the benefits have been proved to be very substantial. Tables 8.3 and 8.4 outline them and in very general terms they can be summarised as:

- greatly improved supervisory control of the plant which in turn enables process optimisation to be implemented;
- elimination of shift to shift changes in the approach to control through the use of a single, consistently-applied control strategy, eliminating the effect of operators' shift changes;
- greatly enhanced process knowledge and understanding.

Figures 8.7, 8.8 and 8.9 showed the improvement in process control achieved through the application of expert systems control. As a result payback periods of considerably less than a year are typical.

Table 8.4 Target benefits for the High Level Control of cement kilns

1	Reduction in standard fuel consumption	5% to 10%
2	Increase in kiln output	10% plus
3	Improved clinker 28 day strength	10% plus
4	Improved clinker grindability	10% to 20%
5	Reduction in milling energy	15% to 30%
6	Reduction in the standard deviation of key process variables	30% to 75%
7	Reduction in average burning zone material temperature	100° to 200°
8	Reduction in peak burning zone material temperature	100° plus
9	Increased refractory life	30% plus
10	Reduction in average kiln exit NO_x level with respect to previous NO_x monitoring periods	50%
11	Increased kiln running times	Positive
12	Percentage run time for HLC	90%

It is also important to consider the disadvantages associated with the technology. In practice, these are limited to the fact that the system demands management commitment in order for the benefits to accrue. The management must also be willing to learn and accept higher standards of process operation which in turn can require higher standards of plant support in order to sustain the benefits.

It can be seen from Table 8.3 that many of the benefits identified so far are due to improved kiln stability and superior, more near optimal, handling of plant disturbances. Figure 8.10, for example, shows the improved level of kiln stability when under computer control on a semi-wet kiln during the latter part of the warm-up period. Once this level of stability is achieved, the management can then use the system to optimise the product quality and

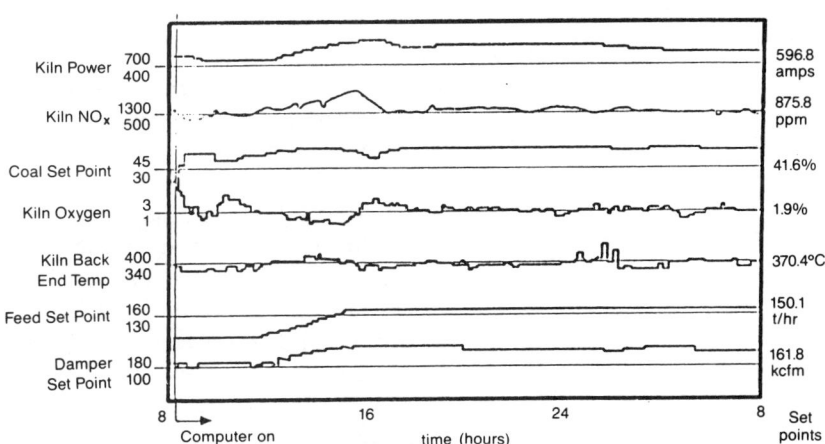

Figure 8.10 Computer controlled warm-up of a kiln over 24 hours

minimise the use of fuel. This optimisation can be very rewarding in that the knock-on effect of improved product quality on the cement milling energy requirements can be significant. The effect of eliminating overburning can reduce the milling energy requirements by up to 30 per cent.

8.13 Discussion

The Blue Circle project points up several important lessons.

Expert systems are a glamorous new technology, which many have said have failed to live up to the expectations that have been aroused. Many expert system applications have been based on commercially produced shells, which have not adequately met the particular needs of the industrial user. Blue Circle investigated the technology, by looking at a commercially available product and deciding that it did not meet their criteria. They had understood the technology well enough to define the system required and collaborate with Sira to design a toolkit, LINKman, which incorporated some of the features of expert systems, but could dispense with others that were not relevant to their needs. For example, they maintained the independence of the knowledge from the inference programs, but did not provide a question answering facility, supplying graphical displays of trends and logs instead.

The continuing success of the project and the replication of the LINKman system on other kilns and mills demands close attention to human factors. Not only must the operators be trained to use the new equipment, but they must also be reassured that their jobs are made more safe by using the new technology. Indeed, were the system to break down or malfunction in some unimagined way, the skills of the process operator remain vital. Abnormal circumstances of the kiln might also require the intervention of the human operator to restore control.

The attitude of management has also been emphasised. The substantial savings that LINKman is capable of yielding could antagonise management, since it could lead to questions from above as to why the plant's management had previously been so poor that such enormous savings had been possible at all. Management's suspicion and fears must be overcome and their support won, the same as for the operators whose hands are on the controls.

The application of expert systems to control of the cement kiln would not have been so successful had it not been for developments in sensors for the industry. On-line measurements of product quality had not been satisfactory, but the advent of reliable NO_x monitors and the demonstrated link between NO_x concentration and burning zone temperature made on-line control feasible. It is hoped that on-line measurement of particle size will make the cement grinding mills amenable to better control too.

The choice of knowledge representation format, If . . . Then rules, was particularly well suited to this application. Mathematical modelling techniques had failed to cope with the large variability of the clinkering process, but human operators had used If . . . Then rules to train each other. A collection of these rules had already been published, so rules were an accepted means of knowledge representation within the industry. The number of rules required to control a wet process kiln is about 70, arranged in four or five blocks. Blue Circle went through a learning phase with 100 to 150 rules. This was too many, so they rationalised them down to a more acceptable number. The published collections of rules were of academic interest only, since Blue Circle preferred to use the process knowledge from their own operators.

One of the oft-stated advantages of rules is their ability to be amended and incremented as the knowledge of the domain increases. That was demonstrated on this project. The manageable number of rules, together with their structure as rule blocks, meant that it was a straightforward task to amend the rules and observe the change in performance of the kiln. Here, the trend displays and data logging facilities were important.

Although the expert knowledge within the controllers was based on that of the process operators, the knowledge was amended under experience. LINKman was the first consistently applied control strategy for long periods of time. Hitherto, changes in the performance of the kiln were confounded with the differences in control strategy of the operators. Hence, it had been impossible to know what were genuine effects of the process and what were due to the operators. A consistent, untiring, automatic controller meant that process effects could be identified and the control strategy amended accordingly. This was an important learning exercise for all involved.

Blue Circle's project on expert systems control of their cement kilns was perhaps not as straightforward as might appear in the above description. At times it was painful, with industrial relations problems causing delays, disappointment and frustration. The very success of the project has created difficulties, not least because the over target savings mean that Blue Circle will have to pay back the grant the Government provided to carry out the project, and no one manager wants it to come from his budget. At the time of the project, Blue Circle was undergoing 'rationalisation', to use the jargon of the time, with the workforce being cut by over a half. Operators, management and research staff were all affected. No-one's job was secure and a successful project on kiln control was not a guarantee of anyone's future employment. However, despite all that, the Blue Circle and Sira teams should be congratulated at seeing the project to a successful conclusion.

Chapter 9 Acquiring knowledge

9.1 Introduction

So far, we have discussed a variety of ways of representing knowledge on computers, manipulating it and using it to control and maintain processes and equipment. But, the overriding question is where does the knowledge come from?

Knowledge acquisition is the process of hunting down the knowledge from whatever source that will be needed for the expert system. *Knowledge elicitation* is a sub-area of knowledge acquisition, concerned with eliciting knowledge from experts. *Knowledge engineering* consists of elicitation followed by coding the knowledge in the knowledge base. The person who does this is the knowledge engineer.

This chapter will look at some of the techniques for elicitation and acquisition, with particular attention to the need of the process control industry.

9.2 The Feigenbaum bottleneck

Knowledge acquisition has been called the 'Feigenbaum bottleneck', after the AI scientist Edward Feigenbaum who declared that it would be the main source of difficulty in constructing expert systems. 'The biggest bottleneck that the knowledge engineers currently face in knowledge acquisition is the great research problem that AI laboratories must face and solve in the coming decade.' Since that gloomy statement appeared in the literature, expert systems have continued to appear, having designed their way around this problem.

Originally, it was expected that expert systems would depend upon experts to supply the knowledge in the knowledge base. This created several areas of difficulty, because

- experts are too busy to spend time being interviewed by a knowledge engineer;
- experts might be suspicious that an expert system could do them out of a job;
- experts do not know what their skills are and might not be able to express them;
- even if they know, they might not want to express them, fearing loss of status and mystique;
- the knowledge representation format might not be well matched to the expert's expertise;
- the knowledge engineer and expert do not know what knowledge the expert system needs.

These are a few of the problems that can occur. Many more are possible. These difficulties all suggest that it would be wise not to rely completely upon the cooperation of an expert.

Furthermore, it turns out that expert systems which rely completely upon expert-supplied knowledge had other difficulties too:

- if more than one expert contributed, disagreements and contrasting styles made unification of the knowledge difficult;
- explanations generated from rules were not always satisfactory.

Various solutions to these problems evolved. Research effort examined the different kinds of knowledge that experts and expert systems might be expected to use, so that the most appropriate and therefore efficient knowledge acquisition technique could be applied in each circumstance. Automatic techniques for acquiring knowledge were developed, such as induction and learning. Other knowledge representation formats and inference techniques appeared, which could represent the first principles or background, textbook knowledge that is important when an expert communicates the solution of a problem to an enquirer. We should not overlook other more esoteric methods for knowledge acquisition such as neural nets and self-organising controllers.

Psychological models of learning, or knowledge acquisition by the expert, propose that learning is a three-stage process:

- the apprentice learns by instruction and observation what actions to carry out in particular circumstances;
- the actions learned in stage 1 are practised until they become accurate and expert;
- actions are 'compiled' through practice until they can be done 'without thinking'.

As Berry states:

Declarative knowledge thus gets transformed into procedural form. As the same knowledge is used over and over again in a procedure we lose our access to it and thus lose the ability to report it verbally . . . as individuals master more and more knowledge in order to carry out a task efficiently they also lose awareness of what they know. Those who have acquired substantial skill in a task . . . generally lose awareness of the basis for their expertise.

This has serious implications for the construction of expert systems, further encouraging the shift away from relying on experts to provide the knowledge. However, techniques exist to help.

This chapter will address that range of problems. The next section reviews briefly some of the knowledge elicitation techniques commonly applied. The following section outlines induction and the final section reviews recent work on learning.

9.3 Techniques for knowledge elicitation

Psychological testing has created a range of techniques over the years for discovering what an expert knows. Some have more relevance to expert system design than others. We shall concentrate here on those most likely to assist in expert systems for process control.

Knowledge acquisition techniques may be divided into two classes – direct and indirect methods. Direct methods rely upon the expert to express directly their knowledge, whereas indirect methods observe other behaviours of the expert, allowing the psychologist to infer what the expert must have known in order to behave in that way. No single technique guarantees success. The wise knowledge engineer will make use of as many as suit the problem. *See* Table 9.1 for some suggestions on matching knowledge elicitation technique to kinds of knowledge.

Table 9.1 Knowledge elicitation techniques and kinds of knowledge

concepts and relations	tutorial or lecture
	reportory grid method
routing procedures	protocol analysis
	task analysis
facts and heuristics	incidental protocols
	memory probes
	structured interviews
classificatory knowledge	sorting tasks
	multi-dimensional scaling

The success of any of these techniques depends upon the goodwill of the expert. As explained above, experts have good reason to feel suspicious of knowledge acquisition, but might also be persuaded to feel flattered that the organisation feels their expertise to be so precious and useful that it is worthwhile investing time and money to capture it for posterity. Experts who are on the point of retirement can feel benignly cooperative for reasons like this.

Interviews

The knowledge engineer conducts an intensive interview with the expert, encouraging the expert to describe the concepts he/she uses, how they are connected together in the mind and the considerations that are made when reaching a decision.

The interview session would start with a wide-ranging review of the expert's domain, perhaps in the format of a lecture or tutorial given by the expert, with a few free-form questions asked by the knowledge engineer. This establishes the vocabulary and concepts the expert uses. The expert should be encouraged to recall particular cases, with special or interesting features. The order in which the expert considers issues is important too. The expert should be encouraged to think about objects, their relationships and inferences. The knowledge engineer should find out what information an expert gathers when beginning to consider a case and how these give rise to hypotheses in the expert's mind. For each factor to the problem, how does it affect other factors.

Experts tend to answer questions of this kind by reference to general principles and the configuration of the particular plant or component in question. The knowledge engineer will likely find the knowledge that begins to emerge is a mixture of general principles, facts describing the configuration considered and highly specific knowledge about the quirks of that rig. The interview will move from one kind of knowledge to another, as the expert tries to explain how problems are solved. Not all the knowledge will be easily classified in this way, but some awareness of the structure of the knowledge that is emerging will help the knowledge engineer keep track of the progress of the interview. Otherwise, it could deteriorate into a 'memory dump', bewildering for all participants.

Questionnaires

The loose structure of interviews means that they can elicit much unforeseen information, but they are time-consuming. Once the basic vocabulary has been established, questionnaires can be used to fill out some of the detail. The expert can work on a questionnaire at a time to suit him/herself and can apply a little more introspection to the answers. Questionnaires can be supplied for each variable, asking for details such as range of values, units, things it depends on etc.

Task analysis

The expert is observed solving problems. The knowledge engineer can attempt to record at the time what the expert is doing and thinking, but is under time pressure. Also, the expert's performance can be video-taped, so that the cases may be reviewed later, with the expert trying to recall what was going on and explaining the thinking that accompanied the actions.

Protocol analysis

Similar to the above, except that the expert is encouraged to think aloud while carrying out the task. The knowledge engineer can support this analysis by asking the expert questions at the time, to try to keep the expert on the right track.

This can be a useful technique for some tasks, but for highly skilled process control tasks, it might not be appropriate. Psychological evidence shows that the area of the brain used during the execution of these tasks is not closely related to the areas used for language and speaking. Hence, having to speak while performing such a task can severely distort the expert's performance. Hence, the expert could perform in a sub-optimal way and give misleading rationalisations of what he/she is doing.

Protocols obtained in this way can be analysed to discover the concepts the expert uses, the facts available and the inferences performed.

Reportory grid analysis

Reportory grid analysis is founded on the psychology of personal construct theory. This proposes that people understand the world in terms of constructs, placing all their known experience within their own personal framework of constructs.

A reportory grid session begins with the expert being asked to name a few important concepts within the domain. The expert is presented with three of these concepts and invited to suggest an attribute that distinguishes one from the other two as a pair. The expert should indicate which of the objects may be rated as 'high' or 'low' in terms of that attribute. The process is repeated until the analyst feels that the major dimensions of the expert's thinking have been elicited. A table is drawn up, which the expert completes, giving the rating of every item against every dimension. This grid can then be analysed to discover how the concepts are related to each other and how the *constructs* correlate on assessing concepts.

This technique needs the assistance of computer programs to process the data. It can reveal subtle knowledge of which the expert is unaware, consistent with its original use in clinical psychology. It suffers from the drawback of drawing on highly personal and individual styles of understanding the world. So although it can assist the expert to learn how to introspect, the knowledge it elicits might not be supportable within an expert system, since it has no rational foundation in the tangible world outside.

9.4 Induction

Induction is a technique for deriving general rules from specific examples. Suppose every computer programmer we've ever met had blue eyes. The process if induction would give us the rule 'If x is a computer programmer, then x has blue eyes'. Contrast this with deduction. Given the above rule and the fact that Ted is a computer programmer, then one could deduce that Ted has blue eyes.

Computer-based induction takes a set of training examples, where each example is described according to several attributes and its classification given. From these examples, general rules are induced.

Induction has proved to be very useful in some applications. If an organisation logs case data, then this can be input to an induction program quite simply. An often quoted application was at Westinghouse which used induction to show that many of the tests they were using to identify faulty items were redundant and millions of dollars could be saved by eliminating these pointless tasks.

However, induction has drawbacks too. The rules the induction program produces might have very little resemblance to those of an expert. This can lead to problems when the justification for applying a particular rule is needed. Induction relies upon empirical association only and has no causal foundation at all. The case examples need to be complete – some induction algorithms cannot cope with missing or uncertain data. The selection of the cases for the initial training set can have a marked effect on the rulers that are induced. Adding, removing or duplicating a case can cause unexpected changes to the rules. It is also desirable to have rules that are as compact as possible, ie with the minimum number of clauses and hence tests. This makes the execution of the resulting decision tree as efficient as possible.

Techniques have been reported in the literature to make automatic induction useful in domains where the examples are less than perfect. For example, problems can occur where a case is classified one way and another apparently identical case is classified another way. Some induction systems pause to ask for another attribute that would discriminate between the two cases, but in many domains, such as medical diagnosis, this is not a satisfactory solution.

9.5 Learning

The capacity to learn is often cited as the most important characteristic of intelligence and until machines can learn, they cannot be described as intelligent. But just as intelligence comes in many different forms and is difficult to define, therefore, so with learning. Certainly, we can agree that learning is more than just acquiring data – it also involves organising that data into information, adjusting to new concepts and applying the new knowledge to solve problems.

Many pattern classification programs use *parameter adjustment* to learn. These programs classify cases into two or more classes according to a number of different features. When writing the programs, it might be difficult to know how much weight to assign to each of the features, so one way to find the correct weights is to let the program adjust the weights itself on the basis of its experience, even to the point of dropping some of the features entirely. This kind of learning needs to decide when a weight should be increased or decreased, and if so by how much. Too big a change can lead to oscillatory behaviour, but too small a change can mean that learning is too slow to be useful.

Learning by parameter adjustment has a few drawbacks as well. There is no mechanism for acquiring new concepts. Weights may be reduced to zero, thereby losing familiar ones, but other features cannot be generated by the program itself. The program designer would have to experiment with the program by supplying new concepts from outside and monitoring the program's behaviour, perhaps with one concept replaced by another. Further, if an expert system were to be in use with such a parameter adjustment program adjusting its probability values, the expert system's behaviour could evolve in a strange way. One might expect that later in its life cycle, the expert system would only be consulted for the peculiar and rare cases. If the expert system is not being used to advise on the frequency occurring problems, then its parameters would be set under the belief that only the rare cases occur. This difficulty is confined to consultative expert systems but not on-line systems, which are obliged to cope with every decision.

Concept learning programs have been constructed for simple research problems. They use semantic nets to represent facts about the cases presented to them. They work by taking a description of one known example of a concept, such as an Arch, which is used as a concept definition. Descriptions of other examples can be compared against the definition, looking for similarities and differences in their descriptions. These can be used to generalise the original definition. Examples of near-misses can also be compared, ie examples that are close to the definition, but not quite an instance of the concept, such as an arch with the uprights abutting. Near-misses can be compared with the definition, so that it can be restricted to exclude these deviant examples.

Other learning techniques have been investigated, such as *discovery* and *learning by analogy*. Discovery is a form of learning in the absence of a teacher. A discovery program would create new frames and fill in their slots, with each new frame representing a new concept. Occasional guidance might be necessary to help discard strange or useless concepts, but the program could assess the potential usefulness of the concepts itself. The most famous example of a discovery program is AM, which used a few basic concepts of set theory to discover a good deal of standard number theory.

Learning by analogy is another research vehicle at the moment, using many AI techniques. For example, a statement like 'Sue is a wet blanket' passes a duty to the hearer to detect the relevant similarities between Sue and a wet blanket. In order to do this, frames should exist describing Sue and Blanket(wet). Heuristics can be used to transfer knowledge from the Blanket frame to Sue's frame, relying on knowledge about character traits. Analogy is a powerful learning tool, but not likely to be practically useful for some time.

9.6 Concluding remarks

Artificial Intelligence has always thrown a bridge between 'hard' sciences, such as computer science and control engineering, and the 'soft' sciences, such as psychology, linguistics and philosophy. This contrast is never clearer than in the field of knowledge elicitation. The technical problems of designing a knowledge representation format and making it useful have their own challenges, but they are empty shells without knowledge. And the people who know most about the acquisition of knowledge and its nature are the soft scientists.

Eliciting knowledge is a difficult task. The effort of making a verbal report on a task has been shown to change the way in which that task is carried out. One must allow for the possibility that there is no correlation at all between a person's mental behaviour and what it is that they say they are doing, although there is evidence to suggest that the changes are made in a useful direction.

Hence, given that knowledge is difficult to obtain, it is worth maximising its use. So, attention should be paid to re-using knowledge as much as possible. Quite a lot of knowledge for a domain is general or commonsense knowledge, of the kind that any reasonably competent person would be expected to have. It would not be a good use of an expert's time to elicit knowledge of that kind. And, since that knowledge is widely available and widely used, it could be applied, with some degree of modification, to other tasks within the original domain as well as new domains.

But before knowledge can be safely re-used, it needs to represented and structured appropriately. When this is done, prototype expert systems could be constructed relatively quickly, which leads to the possibility of automated knowledge acquisition. Experts find it difficult to explain the expertise 'cold', but are better at what the psychologists call 'cued recall'. Thus, confronted with a prototype expert system, an expert could critique and extend it. So, as our understanding improves of the kinds of knowledge that are needed, so it is likely that automated tools for knowledge elicitation will play a greater role.

Chapter 10 Project selection and the expert system lifecycle

10.1 Introduction

Having decided that expert systems are a good thing, the reader of this book might feel tempted to have a go at constructing one. In this chapter, we warn of some of the difficulties that might be encountered and advise on sensible approaches to constructing one's first expert system. We also address what might happen after the expert system is successfully constructed and installed. This is a subject not usually discussed.

The advice on setting up an expert system project is not intended to overrule standard practice for project management. All the usual managerial considerations apply. This chapter merely adds a few more to that lengthy list.

10.2 Identifying a good expert system project

When choosing the right project for the first expert system, the overriding question should be 'Is there a good expert?' Do not think about the domain in isolation, as in 'Is there a difficult problem that our usual techniques cannot solve?' This approach could lead to disaster, because expert systems will not solve an insoluble problem. They can only help people tackle difficult problems.

Defining the 'good' expert is also a complex problem. Is there an expert whose expertise is widely respected and in demand? Could this person spend time helping to create an expert system? Is this person likely to be interested in helping to create an expert system? Can the expert express his/her knowledge and experience well?

The type of expert system affects the considerations as well. If it is a low-level control system, then the expert's input would be needed to start the ball rolling, but could be improved upon once the system is installed. A fault diagnosis expert system relies more heavily on the expert's knowledge, because each outcome is not encountered quite as often and the expert's ability to articulate is more important.

Some important criteria are listed in Table 10.1, together with their likely relevance for both types of expert system. These criteria can help select the right project, but common sense should also prevail. It is too easy to start the project plan by looking at the tools and shells on offer, instead of looking thoroughly at the problems that might (or might not) be solved.

Table 10.1 Several criteria for choosing a good expert systems project and their relevance in process control

Criterion	Low-level control	Fault diagnosis
The task requires expertise and it is available	quite	very
There is a need to capture the expertise or few experts exist	very	very
Algorithmic techniques are not satisfactory	very	very
Symbolic representation and reasoning are used to do the task	quite	very
Heuristic knowledge is important	very	quite
A respected and recognised expert(s) exists	quite	very
The expert is willing and able to help	very	very
A reasonable payoff is expected	very	very
The expert's task is not too easy; it takes more than a few minutes	not	very
The expert's task is not too difficult; takes less than a few hours	very	very
The task is well-defined and well-bounded; likely only a part of expert's job	very	very
A system performing a part of the whole task would be useful	quite	quite
Incorrect or non-optimal results can be tolerated	quite	very
The task is decomposable for development	very	very
The task definition is fairly stable	very	very
The real-time response requirements will not require extensive effort	very	quite
The user interface is straightforward	very	very

When choosing the right project, it is important to define clearly what the expert system will do. Define the role of the expert system, whether as a help, subservient to the expert, or an automatic device which functions under the expert's supervision.

For a first project, don't tackle something too difficult and complex. Expert systems are still under research, so do not venture into the choppier waters, where many difficulties lurk to capsize the unwary. On the other hand, choosing a project that is too simple could produce an expert system that appears laughably obvious. Careful judgement is required here. Expertise that is carefully guarded and revered as a black art might actually be trivial when investigated properly and encoded within an expert system. Such domains are best avoided, because their simplicity makes the system builder look silly, while antagonising the expert who has lost status as a result and is also keen to disparage the concept of expert systems. Domains of that kind might be difficult to identify beforehand, but if a sizable payoff could result, then they are worth tackling.

The knowledge-base should not exceed a hundred rules or so, for the first project. This will mean leaving some knowledge out of the expert system, but it could be successfully incorporated in project 2. Also, many different types of knowledge will be uncovered – stick to the knowledge that is best represented in the format available.

Related to these issues is the well-boundedness of the project. Once the project is underway, it is easy to become entranced by the technical challenges. There is always the temptation to extend the knowlege base just a little bit beyond the original specification, or enhance the user interface with another small but very useful feature. The first project should be regarded as a working prototype, as an exercise for generating ideas that might be implemented in the second project. But the second project will only come about if the first one succeeds and is seen to succeed.

No expert system is going to reproduce exactly the complete behaviour of an expert, at least in the foreseeable future. The expert system will not be up to the expert's standard for some activities, but is likely to outperform on criteria such as reliability and consistency. So, following on from the previous paragraph, if it is possible to bound the task, then one should seek to establish levels of performance that the expert system should accomplish. After all, experts are not expected to be infallible, so neither will be the expert system. Testing and validation will be covered further in a later section.

Again, in order to keep the project feasible, the more peripheral features should be minimised. This can include some additions to the user interface. This is the part of the program that everyone sees, so it is a good idea to make sure it looks acceptably smart and is reasonably simple to use. So, in order to reach acceptable levels of usability, it is important to concentrate on those aspects of the user interface that are absolutely necessary. As discussed in the examples of Chapter 6, managing real-time hypothesis generation can be a tricky business, so again it is wise to keep the real-time parts of the problem as simple as possible.

10.3 Choosing the right tool

Many expert system tools are available on the market, from simple shells that run on a personal computer, to expensive, complex suites of software running on specialised hardware. For a first project, the latter would not be advised. Potential users can view such tools and equipment at the conferences and exhibitions which are currently enjoying such popularity. A few clubs have been established whereunder various companies support the development and installation of an expert system, so that all may benefit from the experience gained.

When exhibition expert systems are seen for the first time, they can be very impressive. The would-be buyer needs some guidance in deciding which is the tool for his/her problem. The previous section has outlined some of the criteria for choosing the right problem; now we need to examine the criteria for choosing the right tool (*see* Table 10.2).

Many of the questions in Table 10.2 require the would-be expert system builder to look carefully at the application. A balance has to be struck between what can be accomplished using the tools available, and not letting oneself be carried away by a flashy tool that holds out the promise of more facilities than are really worth trying to implement. While caution is to be advised, one should not make the mistake of investing in a tool that is underpowered, because this could lead to a poor impression of what the technology could accomplish. A good guide is to choose the project and the tool so that six months should complete the job.

Table 10.2 Choosing the right expert systems tool

Can the tool be easily obtained and installed?
How well is the tool supported by the manufacturer?
Is this likely to continue during the lifecycle of the system?
Will later upgrades be compatible?
Is the current version of the tool stable?
How difficult is the tool to expand or modify?
Is source code available?
What kinds of knowledge representation schemes are provided?
Do these match the intended application?
Can the tool be integrated with other software packages?
Can the tool handle the expected form of input data?
Do the inference techniques match the application?
Is a blackboard provided, if required?
Does the execution speed match real-time, if required, for a realistically sized problem?
Is it possible to produce many copies of the developed system cheaply?

Frame-based tools tend to be more expensive than rule-based and take longer to learn. So a project using frames will get off to a slower start, but its outcome is likely to have a longer life-time. Rule-based systems are good for smaller projects, typically where an apprentice could learn the ropes within a few weeks. There are some problems which rule-based systems can not tackle, such as trying to model reality and reason about it. Frame-based systems would be needed to tackle that, although perhaps augmented with rules for local problems. For a first project, a frame-based system might be too big a bite. It might be better to use a rule-based system on a suitable, modest project in order to get some experience of what can be achieved, so that the experience can be successfully carried over to the next, larger project.

10.4 The six month project

Introducing a new technology to an organisation carries risks for all the participants in the project. There is an ancient Chinese saying which goes something like: 'Success has many fathers. Failure is an orphan.' If a project goes well, everyone will claim a share of the credit, but a failed project has no backers at all. Hence, one must plan carefully to minimise the risks of the project failing and the consequent impact on one's own credibility within the organisation.

A new technology is best viewed as applied research, since many of the techniques will be new to the organisation, so there will be a substantial effort in training the work force and managers to the different attitudes. So, one has to determine the organisation's attitude to funding applied research. Since we are aiming to have a working expert system in about six months, then a minimum of six person-months is required. If the organisation can't or won't fund than much, than the whole idea is best forgotten.

A senior manager is required to support the project through the early funding and planning stages. Identify the AI champion in the organisation, who can help with political support and budget planning. Apart from the six person-months, a substantial amount of money will be needed for buying software and training. It is wise to keep some money for consultancy support too. An external expert systems expert can help the project get off to a good start and save a lot of time and tears later.

The first project month should be spent picking the expert system tool and the application, and writing the project plan. The next two months should be spent getting the first prototype up and running, no matter how rudimentary. The fourth month should be spent reviewing what's been done and what to try next. The working prototype is invaluable in getting feedback from potential users and experts on what their requirements really are. The fifth month will be spent finishing the expert system and the final month in preparing the documentation and installation. Review meetings should be held every month or so. At the end of the project, the team should record their impressions and experiences for the next project (*see* Figure 10.1).

With an unfamiliar technology, it is not easy to tackle a fixed-cost project as outlined above, since one is not very clear about what will be accomplished at the end. However, it has the advantages of limiting the potential damage and focussing the team's minds on what can be achieved. At the start, the objectives are known and can be adjusted as the project progresses and experience gained.

Little published material exists on how to estimate the time for constructing a knowledge base, especially for real-time systems. Schwartz provides some advice for the fault diagnosis type of system, as follows. He recommends building a prototype to cover

Month	Activity
Month 1	Decide application; Choose ES tool; Write project plan.
Month 2	Write first prototype;
Month 3	Run and demonstrate prototype.
Month 4	Review progress so far; Plan next stage; Obtain feedback from experts and users.
Month 5	Finish expert system.
Month 6	Write demonstration; Install expert system; Team reviews lessons.

Figure 10.1 The six month project

the 10 hardest cases that the expert system is expected to manage. The time required to set up these 10 cases can be used to estimate the Average Time Per Case (ATPC). If using a frame-based system, the time to add each further case will be between 0.5 to 0.75 ATPC, ie between 50 per cent and 75 per cent of the time required for one of the original cases. For a rule-based system about 0.75 to 1.75 ATPC. For the next 10 or 20 cases, their time will be on the low side of this estimate and can sometimes be added very quickly, but then it will increase dramatically. At this point, the knowledge base should be re-organised and divided into smaller knowledge sub-bases.

Apart from the knowledge-base, there is also the time for developing the user interface. That will add an overhead of 20 to 40 per cent. If the system has to interface to existing software, add another 20 per cent if you have not done such an interface before.

Other overheads include the time of the other people involved, such as managers. For six person-months of knowledge engineer's time and three person-months of expert's time, add about 1.2 management person-months. Trainee knowledge engineers can be useful too, for some of the programming and documentation. Depending on their level of experience, add 0.25 to 0.5 of a trainee for each knowledge engineer. Users will also need to be included, since their approval is necessary for success. Allow about 0.1 user-month per knowledge engineer's month.

These estimates are based on the myth of the person-month, but at least they are better than no estimates at all. They will help the would-be knowledge engineer estimate the size of project that can be completed with the time and resources that are likely to be available, again helping to present a coherent case of what can realistically be achieved.

10.5 Validation

Intimately connected with all that has gone before in this chapter is the concept of validation. The purpose of validation is to determine that a system performs with an acceptable level of accuracy. (This should not be confused with verification, which determines whether the system correctly implements its specification.) An expert system in not the same thing as an expert, but there are similarities. To what extent should we expect professional behaviour from an expert system?

Validation has usually been attempted in a rather *ad hoc* manner. Often it consists of running a few unseen cases through the expert system and comparing them with an expert's judgement. There are several problems with such an approach. The test cases may not have been well selected and there might not be enough of them. The assessment of the expert system's performance is subjective and subject to bias. The techniques can be formalised and made more objective.

What to validate   Not only should the final conclusion of the expert system be checked, but also its intermediate results. The reasoning process of the system should be checked to ensure that it performs in a sensible way. It would also be worthwhile to check the contents of the knowledge base itself.

What to validate against   The expert system's conclusions should be validated against known results or an expert's performance. If an expert system is expected to diagnose faults, it could be presented with data from an historical case and its response checked. In addition, its performance could be compared with that of the expert under the same conditions.

Choosing test cases   The choice of test cases can easily bias the results. Most importantly, the test cases *must not* have been used in the construction of the expert system. When the expert system project is being drawn up, one must decide whether it should be expected to cope with the most difficult and complex cases, or whether it should cope with the straightforward cases, leaving the expert available to concentrate on the difficult cases. The test cases should be chosen to cover a wide range of expected inputs, as with any software testing and verification exercise. Genuine cases are to be preferred, but if synthetic cases only are available, they will have to do.

Stage of development   The requirement of validation will vary at different stages. In the early days, it will be more important to check on the reasoning processes and the intermediate results, but later, the final conclusions and contents of the knowledge base are important.

Cost of validation   One should also be mindful of the cost of validation. The purpose to which the expert system is to be put will help focus validation. Small expert systems with fairly trivial roles would not require a lot of validation, but an expert system for controlling expensive or hazardous plant would be validated to much higher standards.

Using a validating team   To try to eliminate bias, a separate team of testers should be used to assess the expert system's output. The expert system developers and sympathetic experts can introduce bias, as can hostile experts. A variation on the Turing test might be used here. The team could be given case conclusions produced by both the experts and the expert system. The team could assess them all, trying to identify who produced which.

At the start of the project, crucial decisions need to be made about the range of performance from the expert system that would be acceptable. For a first project, it is better to choose a domain where 100 per cent accuracy would not be required.

Table 10.3 Identify some of the errors that an expert system might make and specify their probabilities

p(*'Expert System Diagnosis'*|*true state of the world*)	Probability
p('Flat Battery'|flat battery)	close to 1
p('Engine About to Blow Up'|engine about to blow up)	close to 1
p('Flat Battery'|engine about to blow up)	close to 0
p('Engine About To Blow Up'|flat battery)	close to 0

It is also important to look at the types of errors that would or would not be acceptable. For example, suppose there were two conclusions that the expert system might produce, Flat Battery and Engine About To Blow Up. In view of the quite different risks associated with the two conclusions, it is worth considering the consequences of the expert system making a wrong conclusion. If it says that the engine is about to blow up when really the battery is flat, then some unnecessary inconvenience is likely to result. The driver might arrange for the car to be checked and organise alternative transport. However, if it tells the unwary driver that the battery is flat, when really the engine is about to blow up, the consequences could be much more severe. Driving off, after fixing the battery, could lead to more than unnecessary inconvenience. At the stage of specifying the project, acceptable levels of probability should be established for the possible errors, and the test cases chosen accordingly. Table 10.3 gives some examples of probabilities that would need to be considered. The first two probabilities in the table are of the expert system working correctly, and would need to be quite high. The third and fourth probabilities are of cases where the expert system has given wrong answers, eg the probability that the expert system diagnoses 'Flat Battery', when really the engine is about to blow up. These probabilities ought to be very low.

Apart from the kind of error discussed in the previous paragraph, there is also the kind of error to do with whether the user accepts the expert system's conclusions (*see* Table 10.4). If a system is valid and the user understands that it is valid and uses it correctly, then the expert system will be a useful piece of equipment. If the system is not up to the standards of validity as specified for whatever reason, and the user understands that, then the project would be best abandoned as unsatisfactory. These two scenarios are correct, but there are two more which lead to errors.

Table 10.4 Errors of responsibility

| | Builder Supplies | |
	Valid system	Invalid system
User accepts as valid	correct decision	builder's liability
User rejects as invalid	user's negligence	correct decision

If the system is valid, but the user declares it invalid, then the user is making an error. In this scenario, it might appear that the user is merely giving himself the expense of a wasted project, but the consequences could be more severe. If the expert made a faulty decision, which had severe consequences, but it could be shown that the expert system would have made the correct decision, then the user of the expert system is at fault for not taking the system's advice. Another scenario could be where the system is not valid, but the user accepts it, believing it to be valid. If the user now acts on the system's advice, there is no guarantee that the advice is correct. A faulty action recommended by the expert system could leave the builder of the system open to blame. In the previous scenario, the user was open to blame for not using the expert system.

These two scenarios depict risky situations, where either the system builder or user could be at fault. While the legal obligations are still vague, it is in the interests of system builders and users to establish acceptable levels of risk, determine the objective standards of performance that the expert system should reach and provide adequate testing of the system. Recent changes in the law concerning product liability and negligence mean that questions on the responsibility of the suppliers and users of expert systems will have to be seriously considered.

When people consult an expert, they expect certain standards of behaviour from the expert. These include:

- not giving a judgement on a matter for which they are not qualified;
- considering all the relevant aspects of the problem;
- using the best data available and carrying out further tests when necessary.

It is still a matter of debate to what extent such standards could be expected of an expert system. Given that users tend to anthropomorphise computers (ie believe that they are more capable of human powers than they are), there is a responsibility to train users in what an expert system can do. All this requires a recognition of realistic and achievable standards of performance from the machines. Not only is there the possibility of inadequacies or bugs in the knowledge base and inference engine, there could also be the more usual problems of hardware faults.

It can be just as bad not to use available technology as it is to rely on a system when you should be using your own head.

10.6 The expert system in use

Expert system technology is still quite new and so most of the literature so far concentrates on the technical issues of designing the expert system, such as the knowledge representation, inference mechanisms and user interface. People are still acquiring experience of how to design a good expert system, so reports on what happens after the expert system has been installed are still thin on the ground. We can, however, offer a few pointers on what to expect.

First of all, do not expect glory. If the expert system is poorly designed, difficult to use and addresses the wrong problem, then it will be the butt of jokes. On the other hand, if the preceding advice has been carefully noted, the expert system might be reasonably good and useful. In that case, it will disappear.

Let me explain how and why it will disappear. For low level process control, the system will become part of the everyday controlling and monitoring of the process. With a carefully managed installation, the system will just be another component of the equipment and the fact that it is designed in a novel way will soon be forgotten. Its actions will have been thoroughly tested and understood by the operators, so it will take its place alongside everything else.

A fault diagnosis expert system will disappear too, but in a different way. In this case, the system is recommending repair or recovery actions to take when a fault occurs. Its advice is consistent and it is capable of some explanation of how its conclusions were reached. The users need never feel embarrassed about asking the same question they asked the day before, having forgotten what the answer was. As a consequence, the users of the system will be able to learn the system's expertise for themselves. The construction of an expert system could mark the first time that a body of knowledge was brought together and expressed in a consistent, usable and accessible manner. It is hardly surprising that it becomes easy to learn. So, the expert system will fall into disuse as the operators acquire its expertise. It might end up only being brought out and dusted off each time a new operator joins the staff.

This highlights one important use of the expert systems that has had regular mention since Chapter 2, as a training tool and medium for storing and transmitting knowledge. Some would believe that this is the most important function of knowledge-based systems and as life becomes more complex and reliant on technology, this may well turn out to be true.

10.7 Concluding remarks

Initiating, planning, carrying out and completing an expert system project is still a novel experience. However, an expert system project is still more like any other kind of project than anything else, so all the usual advice and homilies still apply. Although the computer techniques are new and exciting to the programmers and knowledge engineers, to the users they're just more 'Toys for the Boys'. So, when choosing the project, look very carefully at the application and do not be blinded by the technology that you hope to apply.

Chaper 11 The future of IKBS in process control

11.1 Introduction

Many academic engineers dream of the factory of the future, run only by a man and a dog. The man checks that everything is all right and the dog makes sure he doesn't touch anything. Developments in hardware and software engineering are suggesting how such a thing could come about. Having introduced the basic notions of Artificial Intelligence (AI) for industrial control, we should look at how the techniques could be extended onwards.

11.2 IKBS and industrial control activities

The term 'industrial control' has been used to cover the range of activities from low-level control through fault detection and maintenance to scheduling and planning. So far, we have concentrated on process control and fault diagnosis, but now it is necessary to consider what other knowledge could be used to improve the performance of these and other activities.

For fault diagnosis to proceed effectively, it is useful for the fault diagnoser to have access to the historical record of the development of the fault and some knowledge of the corrective actions that the controller has already attempted. For most current knowledge-based systems (KBS), such knowledge is not available, and the diagnoser must rely upon such data as may be acquired during the consultation by a human operator and input via a keyboard.

Linking the activities of alarm monitoring and fault diagnosis would mean that the location of a possible fault can be determined much more quickly. Many current expert systems start off with little prior knowledge of the location of the fault, which could be anywhere among several components.

Apart from historical data, enhancing the activities of the KBS would require connecting the KBS to more than one component. For low-level control, access to a limited number of sensors and adjustable parameters is sufficient. Rudimentary fault diagnosis may be accomplished using keyboard input, but to link control, alarm monitoring and fault diagnosis together requires an integrated system with connections to several plant components.

Once equippped with extra data inputs, the KBS must be able to use them so as to generate tasks and observe intelligently the behaviour of the other components. For these activities to be possible, the KBS needs knowledge of the interconnections of the components and their behaviour. In other words, the system must contain a model of the plant.

However, the model is not just a physical model of the processes undergone within the plant, but must take account of the classes of component present, the classes of faults which may beset them and the functional behaviour of components (for example that ovens raise the temperature of a given material and change its physical structure so that it may become brittle, aerated or change colour). For particular instances of components, the model should also record individual settings of parameters on the components, its input and output connections, physical location etc.

Equipped with such a model, the KBS would be able to predict how changes in the setting of a valve would show up as a change in process input, for example. If the predicted change were not observed, then there may be a fault in the sensor measuring the change in flow or a fault in the valve. The presence of a corresponding change in process output would confirm that the valve was working correctly, indicating that the sensor was at fault.

It is a short step from the generation of tests and experiments such as these to the possibility of plant re-configuration in response to faults. For example, if a fault is suspected to be due to a partial blockage in a pipe, the KBS could suggest (or implement) a temporary increase in pressure along the pipe in the hope of clearing the fault; or if the fault cannot be repaired without external intervention, the system could take account of any redundancy in the layout of the plant to divert flow along other possible paths. Again, to perform this task, knowledge of the interconnections of the plant must be available.

Once we have a system that can achieve the task of plant re-configuration, it is another short step to scheduling; or if a plant is equipped with a scheduling KBS, it ought to be possible to construct reconfigurations. The main difference between re-configuration in response to a temporary fault and scheduling is the number of components involved in the decision. If flow needs to be diverted round a fault, only a few major components need be affected. Generating schedules requires knowledge of the role of many more of the components within a job shop or chemical plant, for example. Generating schedules for plant shutdown and start-up as the result of a fault could also be undertaken by an intelligent scheduler.

Rather than specifying all possible faults that could occur on a plant, it is more reasonable to look at the kinds of fault that occur on classes of component. For example, pumps could develop leaks or total or partial blockages. If the IKBS knows the component that has detected the developing fault, then immediately the number of possible faulty components can be limited to those reasonably nearby. For example, we might include PumpA in the list of possible candidates. Since there are three kinds of known fault that could affect pumps, we could reasonably suggest that PumpA is leaking or has a partial or total blockage. Thus, we could generate three possible worlds, each containing one fault. These three worlds could be run forward together, comparing them with the real plant. Eventually, some of the candidate faults will show up as bearing little resemblance to the observations, so that they could be deleted from the list. With luck, one candidate will match observations so closely that it will be an obvious explanation of the fault. More likely, several possibilities may suggest themselves as being roughly equal. At this stage several possible techniques exist to resolve the contest between them. If qualitative simulation only has been used, quantitative techniques could be used, taking advantage of the numerical information that may be available from the sensors. Or tests could be generated.

11.3 Qualitative simulation

Qualitative simulation is another area of AI which is currently receiving attention. It is a technique which models the behaviour of physical systems by examining the qualitative changes that occur during a process. As an example, the qualitative changes that are of interest in modelling a bouncing ball occur each time the ball changes direction, that is when it strikes the ground or reaches the peak of its bounce (*see* Figure 11.1).

Qualitative simulation is not concerned with detailed mathematical models and many simulations rely on a three valued logic, where 'zero', 'greater than zero' and 'less than zero' may be the only values of interest. The rates of change of values is also included qualitatively. The lack of mathematical detail means that

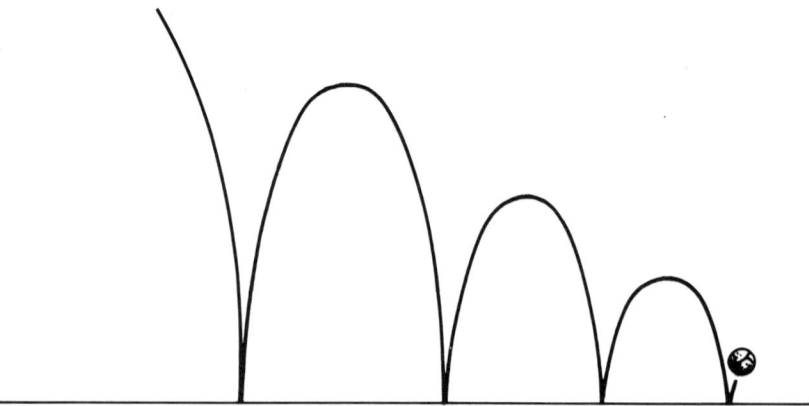

Figure 11.1 Example of qualitative simulation

Qualitative simulation can predict that a ball would bounce, but might not be able to distinguish whether the ball would lose height at each bounce, maintain a level height or gain height with each bounce.

the qualitative aspects of the model may be simulated by the computer very quickly, giving an advantage over mathematical models. However, the lack of numerical detail does mean that the simulation could not distinguish between the validity of a model where the ball kept bouncing to the same height or even gained height with each bounce. The extra inference techniques that would be required to accompany a model to achieve fault diagnosis might be: qualitative simulation, automatic data acquisition, situation assessment, hypothesis list management and test generation.

Scheduling has less interest in process complexity, but could make great use of a plant model. If the frames contained slots describing the capacity of throughput of the component, then when provided with a set of requirements, the IKBS could generate a possible schedule. However, the human scheduler may be aware of temporary disturbances and might want to add extra constraints to the scheduling program, so that particular machines were not so heavily loaded or an important order was fulfilled early. Thus, the scheduler should be able to amend the computer-generated schedule and have the IKBS generate a new one. Once a schedule was implemented, automatic sensors could detect that the schedule is being filled as required or alert the program to impending difficulties on the equipment. If pre-emptive orders come in, the scheduling program could have to adjust again.

The programs surrounding the model would now have to include a schedule generator and constraint matcher, constraint specifier, schedule critiquer and justifier. We add a schedule critiquer and justifier because, at this level of decision-making, the interaction between user and machine has a mixed initiative. We would suppose that the user might want to propose a schedule and have the machine assess it and provide an account of why it considers it to be less than optimal, that is what is often called critiquing. Similarly, when the machine proposes its own schedule, the user would want to know why the machine considers it to be so good. This can help show up the validity of the constraints under which the schedule generator is operating.

When planning involves setting the plant within the economic environment, the executive decision-maker will need a model of the environment. Few satisfactory economic models seem to exist, so again, process models might be required, based on the same sort of If . . . Then rules as were used at the bottom level of process control. But situation assessment is a different problem now, because reliable, scientific sensors do not exist. This problem is usually handled by having the decision-maker postulate a situation and predicting how specified plans would fare under those circumstances. In this way, a plan can be generated that might be robust under several different scenarios. This is sometimes referred to as 'what-if' decision-making.

The other aspect of planning is the design and modification of the plant. The designer may want to specify several different layouts of the plant and consider how each would perform in terms of construction costs, fault propagation, running costs and flexibility. This could be done by providing the designer with a library of components, covering all the pumps, tanks, valves, ovens, wrapping machines and so on that the organisation uses, and thereby enabling the designer to link instances of the components together to form a model of the plant. If the frames contain details of the parts which form a component and their costs, then suitable programs could generate a shopping list of parts. Using simulators similar to those used in diagnosis, the designer could postulate the existence of faults and assess their likely effects, or hand over some initiative to the machine and have it look for possibly catastrophic faults. For this procedure to be useful in practice, the model of the plant would need to run much faster than real time, so that an acceptable speed of response could be provided to the designer.

The use of expert systems for training novice experts has already been mentioned briefly. Once constructed, the IKBS could be modified by adding extra interfaces so that a trainee could learn from an endlessly patient and always available teacher. For example, if we look again at fault diagnosis, when an alarm is detected, the fitter wants a diagnosis as quickly as possible, with instructions on what repair action to carry out. We could call this the 'What now?' mode. Once the panic has died down, the fitter could return to the IKBS and ask for a detailed explanation of how the machine combined observations with its process and plant knowledge to generate a conclusion, the 'why this?' mode. Further, the fitter might have had another idea about what could have gone wrong and would like to supply his/her own explanation for comparison with the machine's, obtaining an explanation of the similiarities and differences of the two diagnoses, the 'why not this?' mode.

11.4 Architecture of the intelligent process control machine

Figure 2.1 depicted the simplest possible expert system, with the knowledge-base separate from the program which manipulates it. In this example, data from the outside world are obtained via a keyboard. Figure 11.2 depicts a much more complex IKBS for process control. Again, the knowledge-base is separate, but is now structured as a hierarchy of classes, with a large range of knowledge held for each class. Instead of just one user interface, there are now several, as well as a host a connections to external sensors and other computers. We shall discuss the physical architecture of the intelligent machine in terms of the sensors, central processor and the user interface terminals.

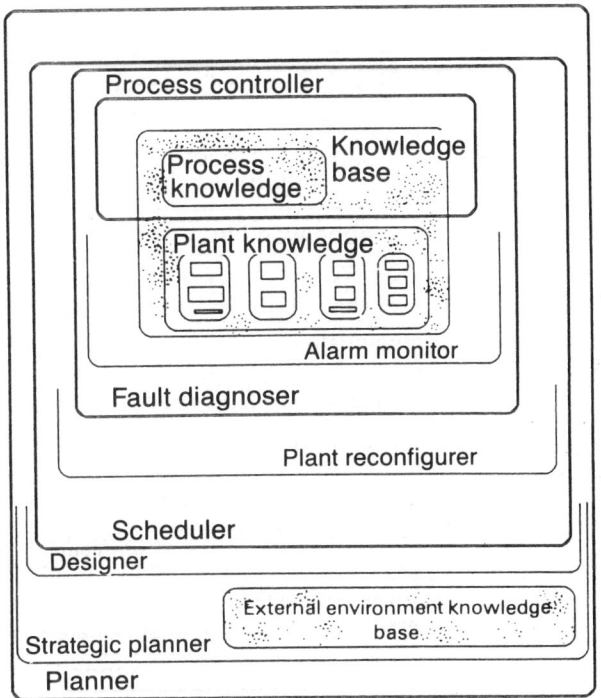

Figure 11.2 A possible configuration of an IKBS for industrial control

Sensors   Sensing equipment is crucially important. We have emphasised throughout that the IKBS should be able to respond in real time, that is at a speed no less than that at which real events occur. Real-time operation would not be possible if the IKBS relied upon human operators typing in all information via a keyboard. Indeed, the success of the expert controllers for cement kilns was partly due to improvements in sensing technology, because data could now be acquired automatically and on-line, whereas hitherto they had depended on operators to recognise the situation.

The data which the sensors gather are used to control particular pieces of equipment. These data would be compared against control rules and control actions generated. For a complete plant, it might not be feasible for all the raw data to be passed to a central processor, which is responsible for calculating the control actions for every individual piece of equipment. If a fault were to develop on that single processor, then the whole plant would shut down.

Instead, each major component of plant would have its own on-board computer, which could serve two purposes. The main purpose is to generate control actions and maintain process output to acceptable levels. The other purpose, proceeding in the background, is to gather statistical data, logging the output of the process, the control actions and so on. The statistical data would be passed to the next level of processing when a fault is detected and the controller can no longer cope; that is when an alarm is triggered.

A third possible purpose for the on-board computer is to do some simple fault diagnosis itself, looking for patterns in the behaviour of sensors, which might indicate a fault in the controller or component, for example.

Alternatively, the computing power could be distributed yet further, by putting a microprocessor within the sensor, so that, when it detects a trend towards unacceptable levels, it passes a message to its mother computer, which responds by looking at the states of other sensors. This could be used as a way of detecting faults in the sensors themselves. Furthermore, recent results in qualitative reasoning suggests other methods for self-testing for sensors. Thus, we could have smart sensors that are self-monitoring.

This processing power within the sensors need not be very special at all. A straightforward circuit with a few chips could do the job. The on-board computer which receives data from sensors could be stand-alone, in that it would not need to be connected to the central processor to operate successfully. It need not be a very sophisticated computer either – BBC micros have already been used for this purpose.

Central processors   Throughout this book, we have referred to the importance of time, so one overriding requirement of the system is that it should operate in real time, that is, the model should run at least as quickly as the real plant. There is little point in its being slower, since events would soon overtake it. There are other requirements that also dictate the design of the IKBS. One is that it should be safe, so that if a fault develops on the processor, the operation of the plant is not in jeopardy. Also, if a fault occurs on the plant, it should be detected and diagnosed as quickly as possible, before dangerous consequences occur. Apart from reliability and safety, the whole system should be capable of being installed in easy stages and on existing plant. Thus, a plant manager might decide to install only smart sensors and no higher intelligence than that, or could install the whole range from control to planning, but only on a very narrow range of components. Therefore, the main requirements are the speed of operation, reliability and flexibility of installation.

These requirements suggest the use of a highly distributed architecture, so that the computing activities are shared amongst many small processors. A single, central processor to handle all the control tasks would be vulnerable, would need to be able to accept many thousands of sensor inputs, should be capable of fast symbolic and mathematical computation, would be expensive to buy and would need to be carefully backed up with an auxiliary processor of equivalent power to ensure continuous operation.

Another advantage of a distributed architecture is that the processor can be tailored to the task it is selected to perform. So, when numerical computation is needed, as on the on-board computers, the appropriate processor is chosen, but when symbolic computation is needed, as for qualitative modelling, then a processor designed for that purpose could be used.

A central processor is still needed, therefore, but if much of the processing is devolved to computers closely attached to the components, then the amount of computation required from the central processor is greatly reduced. Also, the system can be introduced gradually, and enhanced in terms of sensing or central computation as required.

User interface terminals   Apart from receiving and transmitting signals to sensors and controllers, the IKBS must also interact with people, who will be using the IKBS in many different ways through the various interfaces in many different locations, from the peaceful, clean conditions of the research laboratory to the noisy, dusty environment of the plant control room.

Therefore, it is important that the terminals are designed to reflect these differences in use. The controller's terminals might have only a small number of keys or be voice-operated (where possible) to keep the dust out. For fault diagnosis, it might be necessary for the terminal to be light and portable, so that the fitter can carry it round while patrolling the plant. The designer's terminal, on the other hand, can remain fixed in one place, which means that a much more sophisticated display can be used, with colour displays of models of the plant in operation, and several tasks proceeding in parallel. Non-technical or executive staff would need a terminal which is simple and pleasant to use, with the minimum of typing and using menus and icons wherever possible.

Other user interface enhancements are possible. The IKBS could construct a model of the person who is interacting with it at any time, based on their use of the programs, speed of response etc, allowing the IKBS to assess the user's familiarity with the system and expectations from it.

The mixed initiative programs used by designers and trainees should also operate at acceptable rates, since a user will quickly grow frustrated and bored if having to wait more than a few seconds for a response from the machine, underlining the importance of speed of operation.

Feasibility   To assess the design of the IKBS outlined above, one should consider both the hardware and software. The trend in hardware design has been for processors to become cheaper and smaller. Special purpose AI machines are now available from many companies, with central processors designed to achieve speed in symbolic computation. By distributing the intelligence, we minimise the processing effort required of the central processor, so that the machines which exist today could probably achieve what has been outlined above.

However, the software techniques still need to be developed. This work is being done in universities. Further improvements in hardware could help, because less efficient software could be accommodated on faster processors. However, this does not guarantee that the software will be adequately tested and work as expected, so software engineering practice will have to be carefully implemented as well.

Parts of the IKBS described above already exist. The design ensures that the system could be implemented in several easy stages. The feasibility horizon is not far away.

11.5 Concluding remarks

The IKBS described above is intended to suggest a unification of the existing activities within process control. The emphasis has been on symbolic techniques, because we wanted to show where these would be useful. This is not intended to preclude the use of mathematical techniques where they are useful. Indeed, the best kind of system would be one which used both, so that the mathematical techniques are used where precise data are available, and symbolic computation used when most appropriate. Special-purpose processor architecture would ensure that the computation tasks are performed in the most time-efficient manner.

Many people are frightened by the prospect of humans losing employment by the introduction of advanced automation. People are frightened too by the risks involved in managing complex industrial plant, as at Three Mile Island, Flixborough, Bhopal, Seveso and Chernobyl. The ideas expressed in this book are intended to increase safety and efficiency in the operation of complex plant. Only some of the jobs in plant can be replaced by computers, because they are of the sort that humans cannot do well, because of their tedium or magnitude. There are things that humans do better than computers, because of our inherent flexibility and accordingly we have emphasised the role of training, so that workers are given the opportunity to learn from the IKBS, en-skilling rather than de-skilling their jobs.

The intelligent machines outlined above could represent the future automation in industrial control. Parts of what has been described have already been implemented and are being used routinely in industry now. Other parts are the subject of research. The architecture outlined above has been deliberately designed so that it can be introduced piecemeal, a little bit at a time. Industry's caution properly encourages the salami approach to the introduction of change.

However, what has been described is not far from possibility.

References

**Chapter 1
Process control and
Artificial Intelligence**

In contrast to the hype on Artificial Intelligence, the interested reader should instead be encouraged to read some of the more measured texts on the implications of Artificial Intelligence, such as:

M. A. Boden *Artificial Intelligence and Natural Man*, MIT, 1987.

H. L. Dreyfus *What Computers Can't Do: A critique of artificial reason*, Harper and Row, 1972.

J. Weizenbaum *Computer Power and Human Reason: from judgment to calculation*, W. H. Freeman, San Francisco, 1976.

Although some of these books are quite old, their lessons have yet to be fully appreciated.

The Lighthill report makes interesting historical reading now:

Science Research Council *Artificial Intelligence: a paper symposium*, 1973.

**Chapter 2
Introduction to
expert systems**

There are several textbooks on Artificial Intelligence available. Nilsson's book is a classic text, but already seems old-fashioned. Rich's book is a good general introduction to the broad range of AI problems. Feigenbaum and McCurdock's book was both influential and popular. These books describe the expert systems mentioned in the chapter in more detail.

N. J. Nilsson *Principles of Artificial Intelligence*, Tioga Press, Palo Alto, California, 1980.

E. Rich *Artificial Intelligence*, New York, McGraw-Hill, 1983.

E. A. Feigenbaum and P. McCurdock *The Fifth Generation*, Pan Books, 1983.

**Chapters 3, 4 and 5
Knowledge
representation,
Inference and The
Chocolate Biscuit
Factory**

Most books on expert systems tend to be written by academics for their students. Useful, practical books include:

F. Hayes-Roth, D. A. Waterman and D. B. Lenat *Building Expert Systems* Addison-Wesley, London, 1983.

P. Jackson *Introduction to Expert Systems*, Addison-Wesley, Wokingham, 1986.

This is a fast moving field, so it is important to keep up to date with current work. Useful journals are:

Expert Systems, Learned Information, Oxford.

IEEE Expert, published by the Computer Society of IEEE, 10662 Los Vaqueros Circle, Los Alamitos, CA 90720, USA.

International Journal of Artificial Intelligence in Engineering.

Some conference proceedings are also widely respected, such as: British Computer Society Specialist Group on Expert Systems Annual Meeting, published by Cambridge University Press; American Association of Artificial Intelligence; International Joint Conference on Artificial Intelligence; European Conference on Artificial Intelligence.

Chapter 5 is based on an earlier article which appeared as:

> Expert system case study: The chocolate biscuit factory, *Journal A*, Belgian Society of Automatic Control, **vol 27, no 2**, 1986, pp 62–68.

Chapter 6
Interfacing the expert system to the outside world

User interfaces are being taken more seriously lately, but the work is widely distributed. The work of Bainbridge is not well known in the expert system community, but is very relevant. Kidd works on matching the system's inference style to that of the user. A special issue of *International Journal of Man-Machine Studies* contains many stimulating articles, **vol 27, 5 and 6** 1987. *See also*:

> A. L. Kidd and W. P. Sharpe Goals for expert systems research: an analysis of tasks and domains, in *Research and Development in Expert Systems IV*, ed D. S. Moralee, Cambridge University Press, 1987.
>
> L. Bainbridge Ironies of Automation, in *New Technology and Human Error*, eds J. Rasmussen, K. Duncan and J. Leplat, John Wiley, 1987.
>
> L. Bainbridge Mathematical equations or processing routines? in *Human Detection and Diagnosis of System Failures*, eds J. Rasmussen and W. B. Rouse, New York, Plenum Press. pp. 259–286.
>
> L. Bainbridge Diagnostic skill in process operation. Proceedings of International Conference on Occupational Ergonomics, Toronto, May, 1984.
>
> D. C. Berry and D. E. Broadbent Expert systems and the man-machine interface, *Expert Systems*, **vol 4, no 1**, pp 18–27.

Chapter 7
Fuzzy rule-based control

Lotfi Zadeh originated the field of fuzzy sets, and the following paper has stimulated the interest of many researchers:

> L. A. Zadeh Outline of a new approach to the analysis of complex systems and decision processes, IEEE Transactions on Systems, Man and Cybernetics, SMC-3, pp 28–44, 1973.

Rule-based control originated in the early seventies with the work of Mamdani and colleagues. Since then, several theses have been written on self-organising control, while applications of the rule-based controller have appeared. Sugeno's book is a good source of applications.

> M. Sugeno *Industrial Applications of Fuzzy Control*, North-Holland, Amsterdam, 1985.

E. H. Mamdani, Advances in the linguistic synthesis of fuzzy controllers, *International Journal of Man-Machine Studies*, **vol 8**, pp 669–678, 1976.

T. J. Procyk A self-organising controller for dynamic processes, PhD thesis, Queen Mary College, University of London, 1977.

T. Yamazaki An improved algorithm for a self-organising controller and its experimental analysis, PhD thesis, Queen Mary College, University of London, 1982.

E. Lembessis Dynamic learning behaviour of a rule-based self-organising controller, PhD thesis, Queen Mary College, University of London, 1984.

K. Sugiyama Analysis and synthesis of the rule-based self-organising controller, PhD thesis, Queen Mary College, University of London, 1985.

Some of the material in this chapter appeared in the author's article in:

Approximate Reasoning in Intelligent systems, Decision and Control, eds E. Sanchez and L. A. Zadeh, Pergamon, Oxford, 1986.

Chapter 8 Blue Circle case study

Much of the material in this chapter is drawn from previously published articles. The author gratefully acknowledges permission to use them and refer to:

D. W. Haspel The role of rule based control in the process industry, in *IChemE – Advances in Process Control II*, pp 141–155.

J. C. Taunton and D. W. Haspel Rule based expert systems – An application in real time process control and optimisation, presented at Second International Conference on Expert Systems, Sept/Oct 1986, London.

D. W. Haspel, A. D. J. Lorimer, C. J. Southan and R. A. Taylor Blue Circle high level kiln control, presented at IEEE conference, San Francisco, May 1987.

D. W. Haspel and J. C. Taunton, High level control of cement kilns; A practical example of real time expert system technology, IEE one day symposium, 7 December 1987.

D. W. Haspel, C. J. Southan and R. A. Taylor The benefits of kiln optimisation using LINKman and high level kiln control strategies, to appear in *World Cement*.

Chapter 9 Acquiring knowledge

Burton *et al* compare knowledge elicitation techniques in:

A. M. Burton, N. R. Shadbolt, A. P. Hedgecock and G. Rugg, A formal evaluation of knowledge elicitation techniques for expert systems: domain 1, in *Research and Development in Expert Systems IV*, ed D. S. Moralee, pp 136–145, Cambridge University Press 1987.

Another relevant paper in the same volume is:

G. N. Gilbert Question and answer types, pp 162–172, 1987.

Another very practical paper is:

M. Davies and S. Hakiel Knowledge harvesting: A practical guide to interviewing, *Expert Systems*, Feb 1988, **vol 5**, **no 1**, pp 42–49.

See also:

J. R. Olson and H. R. Reuter Extracting expertise from experts: Methods for knowledge acquisition, *Expert Systems*, **vol 4**, **no 3**, pp 152–168.

Information on the commercial process control expert systems can be obtained from a variety of sources *see* Further information section in this chapter.

Chapter 10
Project selection and expert system lifecycle

For an interesting discussion on formal problems of using expert systems *see*:

R. A. Young Expert systems and expert opinion, in *Research and Development in Expert Systems IV*, ed D. S. Moralee, pp 153–161, 1987.

Selecting a good project is discussed in:

S. K. Goyal, D. S. Prerau, A. V. Lemmon, A. S. Gunderson and R. E. Reinke Compass: an expert system for telephone switch maintenance, *Expert systems*, July 1985, **vol 2**, **no 3**, pp 112–124.

D. Prerau Selection of an appropriate domain for an expert system, *AI Magazine*, **vol 6**, **no 2**, Summer 1985, pp 26–30.

O'Keefe has written widely on expert system validation. For example, *see*:

R. M. O'Keefe, Osman Balci and E. P. Smith Validating expert system performance, *IEEE Expert*, Winter 1987, **vol 2**, **no 4** pp 81–98

Some of the legal issues in the use of expert systems are discussed briefly in:

J. S. Zeide and J. Liebowitz Using expert systems: The legal perspective, *IEEE Expert*, Spring 1987, **vol 2**, **no 1**, pp 19–21.

Chapter 11
The future of IKBS in industrial control

Some of the material and diagrams in this chapter appeared in earlier articles:

Knowledge based systems for industrial control, *Computer-Aided Engineering Journal*, February 1987, **vol 4**, **no 1**.

Intelligent machines for process control, in *Creative Intelligences*, eds R. Gregory and P. K. Marstrand, Frances Pinter (Publishers), London, 1987.

Further information

Manufacturers and suppliers

Information on the commercially available process control expert systems can be obtained from a variety of sources, and it will be fruitful to contact the manufacturer or distributor in each case.

- RESCU and COGSYS: S.D. Scicon, Pembroke House, Pembroke Broadway, Camberley, Surrey, GU15 3XD (0276-686200).
- ESCORT: PActel International Centre, 33 Greycoat Street, London (01-828-7744).
- G2 in the UK: Sira Ltd, South Hill, Chislehurst, Kent BR7 5EH (01-467-2636).
- QUIC: Dr. R. Leitch, Department of Electrical Engineering, Heriot-Watt University, Edinburgh EH14 4AS (031-449-5111).
- MUSE: Cambridge Consultants Ltd, Science Park, Milton Road, Cambridge CB4 4DW (0223-420024).
- LINKman: Image Automation Ltd, Kelvin House, Worsley Bridge Road, London SE26 5BX (01-461-5566).
- G2: Gensym Corp, 125 Cambridge Park Drive, Cambridge, MA 02140, USA.
- ART: Ferranti Computer Systems Ltd, Ty Cock Way, Cwmbran, Gwent (06333-71111).

Trade associations

- Gambica, Association for the Instrumentation, Control and Automation Industry, 8 Leicester Street, London WC2 (01-437–0678).
- Electronic Engineering Association, 8 Leicester Street, London WC2 (01-437-0678).
- Computing Services Association, 73/4 High Holborn, London WC1V 6LE (01-405-2171).

Market surveys in AI and expert systems

- Battelle Institute Ltd, 15 Hanover Square, London W1R 9AJ.
- Roland Berger & Partner GmbH, Arabellastrasse 33, D-8000 Munich 81, Federal Republic of Germany.
- Cutter Information Corp, 1100 Massachusetts Avenue, Arlington, MA 02174, USA.
- Databank SpA, Via dei Piatti 11, 20123, Milan, Italy.
- Frost & Sullivan Ltd, Sullivan House, 4 Grosvenor Gardens, London SW1W 0DH.
- Inbucon Management Consultants, Argotill Estates, Oldmixon Crescent, Oldmixon Trading Estate, Weston-super-mare, Avon BS24 9BA.

- International Resource Development Inc, 21 Locust Avenue No 1C, PO Box 1716, New Canaan, CT 06840, USA.
- Mackintosh Consultants Co Ltd, Mackintosh House, Napier Road, Luton LU1 1RG.
- Market Intelligence Research Co, 2525 Charlston Road, Mountain View, CA 94043, USA.
- Ovum Ltd, 44 Russell Square, London, WC1B 4JP.
- Technical Insights Inc, PO Box 1304, Fort Lee, NJ 07024, USA.

Consultancy, applications, software
- Logica Cambridge Ltd, Betjeman House, 104 Hills Road, Cambridge CB2 1LQ (0223-66343).
  Consultancy, research, development and applications of expert systems in a wide range of industries. Experience in Alvey and ESPRIT projects. Wide range of hardware and software tools.
- Sira Ltd, Industrial Systems Division, South Hill, Chislehurst, Kent BR7 5EH (01-467-2636).
  Consultancy, research, development, applications and training for expert systems in process control and manufacturing systems. UK agent for Gensyms G2 system, certified for G2 training, referenced consultant to Intellicorp for KEE applications.
- S.D. Scicon, Pembroke House, Pembroke Broadway, Camberley, Surrey GU15 3XD (0276-686200).
  Consultancy, design and applications of expert systems in industry and defence. Developed COGSYS through a user club activity.
- National Computing Centre Ltd, Bracken House, Charles Street, Manchester M1 7BD (061-228-6333).
  A range of knowledge based systems consultancy, training and training materials, also systems building for external agencies. Awareness through the KBS Circle activities.
- ERA Technology Ltd, Cleeve Road, Leatherhead, Surrey KT22 7SA (0372-374151).
  Advanced software design and implementation for knowledge based systems in industrial applications.

Awareness and club activity
- UK Department of Trade and Industry, Information Engineering Directorate (IED), Kingsgate House, 66–74 Victoria Street, London SW1.
  Responsible for on-going Alvey Programme involving KBS user groups, demonstrator projects, research programmes. New collaborative programme (post Alvey) projects being appraised for DTI and SERC grants. IED also responsible for UK route to ESPRIT, the European programme for collaborative research in

information technology, including expert systems for process control.

IED Switchboard 01-215-7877.

KBS enquiries 01-215-2500.

ESPRIT enquiries 01-215-8340.

– UK Department of Trade and Industry, Manufacturing and Materials Division, 123 Victoria Street, London SW1E 6RB (01-215-7877).

DTI support to encourage uptake of AI/expert systems in manufacturing. Sponsors of joint DTI/BCS annual award for best manufacturing intelligence applications in Britain.

– Association of Independent Research and Technology Organisations, c/o Hellier & Co, 15 Church Street, Ilchester, Yeovil, Somerset BA22 8LN (0935-841-314).

Many members of AIRTO organise workshops and club activities for clients in expert systems awareness and applications.

– COGSYS and RESCU User Clubs, *see* S.D. Scicon above.

– Sira Industrial Expert Systems Club, Sira Ltd, South Hill, Chislehurst, Kent BR7 5EH (01-467-2636).

Over 60 companies participating, claimed to the largest club in Europe. Provides information and guidance on applications, plus hands-on application experience. Reports, workshops, meetings, projects. Formal links with industrial user groups in continental Europe.

Learned societies active in expert systems and process control

– British Computer Society, 13 Mansfield Street, London W1M 0BP (01-637-0471).

– Institute of Measurement and Control, 87 Gower Street, London WC1E 6AA (01-387-4949).

– Institution of Electrical Engineers, Savoy Place, London WC2 (01-240-1871).

– Institute of Electronic and Electrical Engineers, 10662 Los Vaqueros Circle, Los Alamitos, CA 90720, USA.

– Instrument Society of America, 67 Alexander Drive, PO Box 12277, Research Triangle Park, NC 27709, USA (919-549-8411).

– Institution of Chemical Engineers, 12 Gayfere Street, London SW1 (01-222-2681).

Academic research in AI and expert systems

– University of Cambridge, Computer Laboratory, New Museums Site, Pembroke Street, Cambridge CB2 3QG (0223-334600).

- University of Cambridge, Department of Engineering, Trumpington Street, Cambridge CB2 1RX (0223-338100).
- Queen Mary College, Department of Electrical and Electronic Engineering, Mile End Road, London E1 4NS (01-980-4811).
- University of Oxford, Engineering Department, Parks Road, Oxford OX1 3PJ (0865-273000).
- Heriot-Watt University, Department of Electrical Engineering, Edinburgh EH14 4AS (031-449-5111).
- Science and Engineering Research Council, Polaris House, North Star Avenue, Swindon, SN2 1ET (0793-26222).
  SERC fund post-graduate research in UK higher education institutions, including AI/expert systems research.
- Massachusetts Institute of Technology (MIT), Cambridge, MA 02139, USA (617-253-1000).
- Turing Institute, 36 North Hanover Street, Glasgow G1 2AD (041-552-6400).
- Stanford University, Stanford, CA 94305, USA (415-723-2300).
- University of Sussex, School of Cognitive and Computing Sciences, Brighton BN1 9QN (0273-678379).
- University of Edinburgh, AI Applications Institute, 80 South Bridge, Edinburgh EH1 1HN (0224-40241).
- Glasgow University, Computing Science Department, 17 Lilybank Gardens, Glasgow G12 8QQ (041-339-8855).
- Carnegie-Mellon University, Robotics Institute Intelligent Systems Laboratory, 5000 Forbes Avenue, Pittsburgh PA 15213 (412-268-2000).

Index

MEASUREMENT AND CONTROL TECHNOLOGY SERIES

Published in association with the Institute of Measurement and Control, UK

Series editor: T. P. Flanagan OBE MSc FIEE FInstMC FInstP

Fluid flow measurement
   by R. A. Furness

Expert systems in process control
   by J. Efstathiou

Automatic inspection technology
   by G. A. W. West, T. J. Ellis, R. A. Brook and L. Finkelstein